Pilates
made easy

First published in the United Kingdom in 2011 by
Collins & Brown
10 Southcombe Street
London
W14 0RA

An imprint of Anova Books Company Ltd

Text by Zoë McDonald
Pilates consultant: Catherine Royce
Photographer: Caroline Molloy
Model: Sheree Ferreira

Distributed in the United States and Canada by
Sterling Publishing Co, 387 Park Avenue South, New York, NY 10016-8810, USA

Zest is the registered trademark of The National Magazine Company Ltd.

ISBN 978-1-84340-526-9

A CIP catalogue for this book is available
from the British Library.

10 9 8 7 6 5 4 3 2 1

Reproduction by Rival Colour Ltd, UK
Printed and bound by
1010 Printing International, China

This book can be ordered direct from
the publisher at www.anovabooks.com

The exercise programmes in the book are
intended for people in good health – if you
have a medical condition or are pregnant,
or have any other health concerns, always
consult your doctor before starting out.

Pilates
made easy

FROM THE NUMBER ONE WOMEN'S HEALTH MAGAZINE

in association with

ZeSt
MAGAZINE

COLLINS & BROWN

Contents

Foreword

Congratulations on buying this book – if you want a lean, toned and healthy body, you're in the right place!

Not only will Pilates tone up those pesky wobbly bits (it's the secret behind many an A-lister's enviably flat stomach!), it will also improve your fitness and give your energy and wellbeing a huge boost. Plus, it's a great way to alleviate back pain, perfect your posture and improve co-ordination.

But not everyone has the time or money to go to a regular Pilates class, so this book makes it easy for you to practise regularly in the comfort of your home, providing easy-to-follow workouts to suit your goals. The only thing you'll need is a mat! Even if you do take classes or work out with an instructor, as I do, you'll find this book a hugely helpful companion, giving you invaluable guidance and tips and refreshing your understanding between classes.

Every exercise is explained step-by-step and has clear annotated photographs so you can check you're getting it just right. There are beginners, intermediate and advanced workouts to work through, as well as specially designed workouts to target specific problem areas. If you practise regularly, I promise you'll see dramatic results, and fast.

Enjoy and good luck!

Mandie Gower
Editor
Zest Magazine

How to use this book

▶▶▶ This book is designed to help you to master and develop a Pilates routine that can be easily incorporated into your daily life for a healthier, happier and more toned you!

We've tried to make this book as straightforward as possible. Whatever your fitness level, you should start with the basic mat sequence chapter (see page 24), and work from there. Each exercise runs through step by step, with plenty of photographs to guide you along your way, and top tips on how to perfect your practice. It's crucial that you don't race ahead to the more advanced exercises until you're completely confident you're ready. Take your time to read through the instructions fully a few times before you embark on the workout. In Pilates precision is key, so it's important to really focus on each instruction and to stay mindful of everything your body is doing as you exercise. You won't be able to 'zone out' and should feel that your brain has been given a workout at the end of each session.

As you get more competent and confident and as your body gets stronger, you can add exercises from the chapters that follow to form an intermediate and finally an advanced sequence. Rather than following on chronologically, the more advanced exercises slot in to

THE PROGRAMME AT A GLANCE

Whatever your level, you should try to find time for your basic mat sequence at least four times a week. As you get more proficient, when you have time do your intermediate or advanced mat sequence instead.

Beginners wanting to target their apple or pear shapes specifically should do their basic mat and shape sequences together, twice a week if possible (doing the basic mat sequence on its own the other two times).

Those at intermediate or advanced level will find most of the shape exercises in their mat sequence although, when pressed for time, the shape-specific workouts are useful for everybody.

Basic

Intermediate

Advanced

> **Pilates helps you to control your movements very precisely, while engaging and working the body's core muscles. It's important to master this principle by practising the basic exercises carefully, before moving on to the more advanced ones.**

your existing routine at specific points to build up a longer, more rigorous exercise sequence. An updated sequence is listed at the beginning of each new chapter, and the full sequence is clearly illustrated in the pull-out visual guide at the back of this book for handy reference. This offers a purely visual trigger for you to use as a guide during your workout, so you can see at a glance what comes next. To begin with you'll need to follow the written instructions within the book but, once you're familiar with the workout and have memorised the instructions, the fold-out sequence should provide an at-a-glance cue.

Pages 117–21 offer targeted workouts for the two most common body types – the apple and the pear. These workouts are suitable whatever your level and are designed as must-dos for your body type, working as more targeted alternative to your standard mat sequences. You'll be doing some of these exercises in your mat sequence anyway so, even if you don't do the apple or pear workout on a given day, make sure you pay special attention to the exercises that relate to your body type.

The number of exercises in the intermediate and advanced sections might seem intimidating, but, rest assured, once you become proficient the intermediate sequence should take around half an hour, while the full advanced workout should take only 40 minutes. If you're pressed for time, use the basic mat sequence (pages 24–39), integrating the full series of abdominal exercises if you're intermediate or advanced. This should be enough to maintain your powerhouse (see page 14).

THE KIT

For your Pilates workout the only tool you'll need is a proper Pilates mat (thicker than a yoga mat, as it needs to cushion your back from a lot of spinal rolling). If you don't have one, a folded blanket will make a useful alternative.

You should wear comfortable, but close-fitting, clothes . A fitted vest and leggings are ideal as it's useful to be able to see your body as you exercise. If you want to do the arm exercises, you'll need a couple of light hand weights (no heavier than 1–1.5kg/2–3lb). Bare feet are best for Pilates but, if you prefer to keep them covered, opt for socks with grips to protect against sliding. Ballet shoes are another option.

Introduction

Pilates is a system of exercises designed to rebalance, strengthen and elongate the body. Pilates promises longer, leaner, more sculpted muscles, increased flexibility, better posture, improved balance and a strong mind–body connection.

What is Pilates?

INTRODUCTION

BASIC

INTERMEDIATE

ADVANCED

PILATES FOR YOU

▶▶▶ Pilates is a tried and tested method of exercise that has been around for almost a century. Drawing on several other techniques, Pilates requires you to engage your mind to strengthen, stabilise and condition your entire body.

Pilates was created and developed by German fitness enthusiast Joseph Pilates during the early part of the 20th century as a way to strengthen his own body (he suffered from rickets and asthma as a child). Pilates refined his regime to keep his fellow prisoners of war fit during the First World War, helping them regain strength in their muscles through resistance exercises that they could practise in their beds. His method fuses eastern and western exercise philosophy, taking elements from yoga and martial arts as well as boxing and other fitness disciplines. Originally, Pilates called his system 'the art of contrology', a name that demonstrates the importance of mindful movement

through complete mind–body mastery. In Pilates the objective is to train the body to operate functionally, with the muscular and skeletal system working in harmony. It's a re-education for your body, teaching you how to move and 'be' correctly and releasing you from any bad postural habits you've picked up.

A strong mind–body connection is right at the heart of Pilates and the system helps those who practise it regularly to become more physically mindful. It will help you to become more aware of your body, tuning in with it at a very deep level, and to control your movements more precisely, right down to the tiniest muscles.

Above: Strong but flexible – a healthy spine equals a healthy body. Pilates is known for the strengthening and conditioning benefits it can bring to its devotees.

Above: The navel should be pulled inwards and upwards during Pilates exercises.

What are the body benefits?

Fast-forward a century and celebrity endorsements, from Madonna to Gwyneth Paltrow, have also made the conditioning benefits obvious. Aside from the A-list advocates, Pilates is also widely recommended by physiotherapists, chiropractors and doctors for people recovering from injury or trauma. It offers impressive strengthening and conditioning results. Once people discover Pilates, they'll often continue with it for life, as it's one of the few fitness systems that anyone can do, whether they're old, young, flexible or inflexible. 'Pilates develops the body uniformly, corrects wrong postures, restores physical vitality, invigorates the mind and elevates the spirit', said its founder.

Will I need fancy machines or equipment?

The Pilates workout is a series of exercises that can either be done on a mat or with the aid of equipment. In this book, we've chosen to stick with the mat-based exercises, as these are easy to perform at home, and we believe 'mat is where it's at'. Your body is the finest tool imaginable and mat-work forces you to discover where your weaknesses are and to work on them, using your own muscle strength.

How does it work?

In all Pilates exercises the powerhouse is at the centre of movement. This term relates to the muscles that surround the torso, buttocks and back. The objective is to keep them engaged and active throughout all of the exercises. Concentration and getting it right are crucial – this approach isn't about lots of reps or exercising to the point of fatigue. More important are precision, focus and commitment. Give each movement 100 per cent, stay mindful of the six principles of Pilates, and you should only need to do 3–5 reps of most of the exercises.

Tell me more about these six principles

They are:

★ **Centring:** Making sure all movements initiate from the powerhouse
★ **Concentration:** Ensuring you're completely focused in the moment and the movement
★ **Control:** Maintaining mastery over every muscle in your body as you exercise
★ **Precision:** Getting it exactly right, and moving as you intend to move
★ **Breath:** Co-ordinating it with your movement
★ **Flow:** Keeping movements smooth, with one exercise fluidly transitioning into another.

We will explain more about these principles later (see page 22) and give plenty of tips on how to put them into practice.

How fast will I see results?

It doesn't take long to feel and see the benefits of Pilates and, the joy of it is, the workouts don't have to take long. It's all about quality, rather than quantity, so three short workouts per week will bring benefits. Joseph Pilates himself offered this promise: 'In 10 sessions you will feel the difference, in 20 you will see the difference, and in 30 you will have a whole new body'.

The powerhouse

▶▶▶ Your powerhouse is made up of the muscles that surround the centre of your body – all your abdominals, back and bottom muscles. It is in this region that movements should begin, and a strong powerhouse is the focus and key to all Pilates exercises.

INTRODUCTION

BASIC

INTERMEDIATE

ADVANCED

PILATES FOR YOU

Pilates is different from conventional exercise, as it treats the body as a whole. So, rather than thinking of a Pilates exercise as working only your abs, triceps or bottom, if you're doing it properly, your whole body will be working throughout each exercise. The key to this is building a strong powerhouse – your abdomen, lower and upper back, hip, buttock and inner thigh muscles. It's more all encompassing than just the 'core' you hear about in other forms of exercise (often used to refer just to the deepest abdominals). The objective is to keep all these muscles connected and active throughout Pilates.

As you practise Pilates, you will be continually lifting and lengthening, with the power of each movement directing outwards from your powerhouse. There are a few key directions that will help you to keep your powerhouse working correctly and, as a result, will protect your back and neck as you exercise, also ensuring that each exercise works your entire body. Here are some terms to help you visualise what to do:

Scoop
A word we'll use a lot describing how to pull your stomach inwards and upwards, inside your ribcage. Imagine there's a piece of string attached to your navel and that it's being pulled taut towards your spine. This is different to just sucking your tummy in as much as you can – it's more about control than restriction and it's crucial that you continue to breathe naturally. It's also sometimes helpful to visualise this as a zip, running from your pubic bone to your navel. You'll need to keep this 'zip' or 'string' active throughout each exercise.

Lengthen
The long, lean muscles Pilates devotees develop are, in part, a result of the constant stretching and lengthening the exercises require. So you should be aiming to extend your legs long out of your hips and extend your neck long, pulling your shoulders down away from your ears. When you're doing the reclining exercises, your back should always be lengthened flat on the floor (be careful not to force it though by tucking your pelvis under). Imagine yourself increasing the distance between each vertebra as you perform your exercises to keep the length in your spine and waist.

Wrap
A word that should help you to visualise how to engage your buttocks. Rather than just clenching or pinching them, imagine your buttocks are wrapped around your hips. Hold them together as if they're grasping a piece of paper!

Soft
A term used to refer to extended, but not 'locked', elbows and knees. The objective is to lengthen without hyper-extension.

Pilates stance (right)
When you see this in the directions for a position, it means heels squeezed together, toes slightly turned out (although not exaggeratedly so). This is intended to connect the backs of the legs and the buttocks. The feet should 'hang' naturally, as from a skeleton.

Perfect Pilates stance

Long through the
back of the neck

Wide collarbones

Shoulders relaxed

Lats pulling down (behind)

Narrow the waist,
tummy pulling in
and upwards

Buttocks wrapped

Inner thighs drawing together

Heels together,
toes slightly apart

IMPORTANT MUSCLES

★ **Abdominals:** The muscles
running down the front
and sides of your torso that
provide stability.

★ **Transverse abdominals:**
The deepest of the stomach
muscles, running
horizontally around your
torso like a support belt.

★ **Lats:** The broadest muscles
in your back, below your
shoulder blades.

Glutes: The muscles in
your buttocks.

Obliques: The side stomach
muscles that form your
waist. Responsible for the
twisting of your torso and
side stretching.

It worked for me...

▶▶▶ Real people and celebs share why they're so passionate about Pilates.

Tim Richards, trainee teacher, 41

After jarring a disk in a skiing accident 15 years ago, I've suffered bouts of lower back pain. My back would suddenly just go and I'd have to take strong painkillers and walk gingerly for days until it recovered. I tried everything from osteopaths to chiropractors, but nothing stopped these frequent episodes. Then I started going to Pilates every Friday evening. The result was miraculous. It totally changed the way I hold myself and strengthened the muscles around my problem area. I haven't had a single episode of pain since, and I never miss a class!

Nicky Cronin, insight manager, 34

I used to think that Pilates was for old people, but as a recent convert, the more I learn about it, the more I realise this couldn't be further from the truth. The more you practise, the harder it gets. I love the fact that it's inwardly focused and that it's you against yourself. It makes me feel revitalised, and I really look forward to my sessions. A fan for life, I think!

Jennifer Aniston, film star, 42

I'm a Pilates person. It's great. I had a hip problem, a chronic back and a pinched nerve, and it's solved all of it. I love it. It makes me feel like I'm taller.

Gaby Roslin, TV presenter, 46

Pilates has changed my life! I used to wake up each morning, bent over and in pain from my lower back. I used to have physiotherapy every week and each week my physiotherapist would beg me try Pilates. Eventually, as a New Year's resolution, I tried a mat class. From that moment on I was hooked. Two years later I still go every week and I am now a total convert. It has 'fixed' me and for that I will be ever grateful.

Trudie Styler, actress, 57

Pilates has been the perfect solution to maintaining strength and vitality in my life. The varied combination of easy, low impact manoeuvres make this an easy routine that just about anyone can use.

Kate Smart, personal trainer, 40

As a fitness instructor and level 2 Pilates instructor, I was very much aware of the benefits Pilates offered my clients, but rarely found time to practise what I was preaching myself due to work and family commitments. But since attending one or two Pilates classes weekly for six weeks or so, I've become much more mindful of my body. After each class I feel that I move far more freely, especially around my shoulders and hips, and using my core muscles now feels like second nature. I braved a bikini recently and was complimented on my toned tummy. I can only attribute that to Pilates as nothing else in my life has changed.

The lifestyle benefits

▶ ▶ ▶ Pilates isn't just a way of toning your muscles to increase your physical fitness, it's designed to have a positive impact on your whole life by relieving pain, reducing stress, improving sleep and much more.

The best thing about Pilates is that it was developed with an holistic aim: to enable you to move functionally and mindfully at all times and to foster the kind of fitness that will support your body to do the things it needs to do in your everyday life. What's more, the control and mindfulness Pilates helps you to develop reap benefits that go far beyond the physical. You should see a reduction in stress levels and may well find you're sleeping better and even feeling more confident.

Above: Taking even just a short time out from a busy day to practise Pilates can help you to de-stress and find calm and wellbeing.

Here's a little more information on why Pilates has so much going for it:

★ It can work better than medicine
A US study on lower-back pain sufferers found that those practising Pilates for four weeks reported greater improvements than those on conventional treatment programmes.

★ It can improve your performance in the gym or on the pitch
Countless sportsmen and women, from David Beckham and Tiger Woods to Serena Williams, have revealed that regular Pilates forms part of their training regime. The core conditioning and physical control that come with Pilates practice are an advantage to anyone who plays any sport regularly.

★ It's calming
It requires you to slow down, focus, co-ordinate your breath and your movement and to find a quiet time and place for yourself. One study also found that it significantly boosted feelings of wellbeing.

★ It improves your co-ordination
Pilates encourages you to build greater body awareness, and the flowing, sometimes tricky, exercises mean that you'll have to use your brain to ensure you're moving and engaging the right muscles at the right time.

★ It helps guard against or counteract RSI
Even if you don't have RSI (repetitive strain injury), if you spend a lot of time at a computer, or using hand-held devices to text or email, you'll benefit from the stretching in Pilates. The RSI Awareness Website (www.rsi.org.uk) lists Pilates as a worthwhile treatment.

FIVE WAYS TO USE PILATES EVERY DAY

1 Sitting at your desk, scoop your navel towards your spine and pull your shoulder blades down your back. Breathe laterally, allowing your ribs to expand to the sides. Try this whenever you're feeling hunched or stressed as a quick way to counter slouching and shoulder tension.

2 On the bus or train to work, choose to stand and occasionally – with caution – test your balance by slightly releasing the pole or handrail. Use your powerhouse to stabilise you, as if you were on a wobble board.

3 Getting up first thing in the morning, avoid doing the 'mummy lurch' – jerking forwards like a zombie to swing your feet to the floor.

Instead, scoop your stomach to your spine and lead with your chest and arms.

4 Sitting in front of the TV or in the pub, don't cross your legs. Keep your legs in line with your hips, feet flat on the floor and scoop your stomach towards your spine, pulling your lats down as you did sitting at your desk.

5 To ease back pain after a tiring day, do the Rolling Down the Wall exercise on page 125. Whether you're feeling the strain of a long drive or a day spent at your desk, this is one of the most effective way to quickly realign your posture, stretch out your spine and release tension.

Above: When you are sitting at your desk, or on your sofa, remember your posture. You should be sitting with a long straight back, shoulders relaxed, tummy drawn in and hips, knees and feet all in a line.

A note on safety

▶▶▶ Although Pilates has a reputation for being a gentle form of exercise, it is easy to injure yourself if you don't practise correctly. Using your muscles in the right way during each exercise is crucial.

INTRODUCTION

The aim of Pilates is to master your muscles, controlling them exactly as you intend to with every exercise. If you don't, not only will you not see any benefit, you run the risk of overstraining a muscle or hurting yourself.

When you first start Pilates, it may seem like there is an incredible amount to take in, but it's really important to take your time reading through the instructions. As you exercise, try to focus on the six principles of Pilates (see pages 22–23), and mentally run through the checklist (see opposite) during every exercise, to ensure you're doing it properly. This attention to detail is an effort, but one that your body will reward you for.

Be patient

Most importantly, be patient. If you're a beginner, start on the basic exercises and don't be tempted to skip ahead to the intermediate or advanced chapters. Unless they feature in your apple or pear workout (in which case, take note of any modifications), you shouldn't move on to the intermediate exercises until you are 100 per cent confident and comfortable with the basic sequence. This means that you can do every exercise perfectly according to the instructions, in a flowing sequence and are sure you're using the correct muscles.

The sequences in this book are designed to work in order, with many exercises counterbalancing the previous one, as Pilates uses opposition to ensure the body is being trained safely. Omit an exercise only if you experience pain. Listen to your body. However, if you want to focus on particular body parts or have a specific objective in mind (whether that's a quick morning wake-up routine or more toned arms), check out the Pilates For You chapter at the back of the book, on pages 114–25.

INJURY-PROOFING GUIDELINES

★ **Check your mat.** The one investment you need to make is a proper Pilates mat. In Pilates, there is a lot of spinal rolling, so a yoga mat won't offer enough cushioning. When you don't have one to hand (on holiday, for example) you can substitute a couple of folded towels or blankets.

★ **Know pain when you feel it.** If you experience any pain, stop immediately. You should feel your muscles working hard, but if something feels wrong, listen to your body. Many of the exercises in this book have modifications to try if you're experiencing any back or neck pain as you do them. Heed this advice; never be tempted to 'push on through'.

★ **Remember the powerhouse.** The most common mistake people new to Pilates make is that they get so focused on the movement of an unfamiliar exercise, they forget to keep their powerhouse working. Ensuring these muscles are active and engaged is the basis for correct technique, and the foundation for every single exercise in this book.

INTRODUCTION

BASIC

INTERMEDIATE

ADVANCED

PILATES FOR YOU

Child's Pose

One of the counter stretches recommended throughout the book to release your back muscles after you've been working them is Child's Pose. Here's how to do it:

From kneeling, sitting on your heels, take your knees wider than hip-width apart, and round forward, keeping your toes together, either stretching your arms straight out in front of you to get a deeper shoulder stretch, or taking them back towards your feet, palms to the ceiling. Tuck your chin in rounding your back, sinking your tailbone down to the mat. Breathe into the stretch.

CHECK LIST

When practising Pilates exercises, ask yourself:

⭐ Is my tummy scooped towards my spine?

⭐ Are my shoulder blades and lats drawing down towards my hips?

⭐ Are my buttocks (glutes) wrapped?

⭐ Are my inner thighs pressed together?

The six principles of Pilates

▶▶▶ Before you get started, it's important to familiarise yourself with the six fundamental tenets of Pilates, the basic principles that underpin the whole system and approach.

INTRODUCTION

BASIC

INTERMEDIATE

ADVANCED

PILATES FOR YOU

Mastering the six principles is a neverending process rather than a task that you can complete and then move on to the next thing. The idea is that you stay mindful of all of them as you practise (and in your everyday life too, as Pilates is intended as a re-education for your body). So, rather than thinking of it as a checklist to stick to, aim instead to internalise these principles, so that practising them becomes automatic.

1. Centring

The principle of centring is that all movement should be directed outwards from your powerhouse (see pages 14–15). You should start each exercise from your centre so that your body is strong, controlled and 'charged' before you begin to move. This is the key to Pilates.

Above: Place your hands on your ribcage. Note how the ribs must expand outwards to the side on the inhale and knit together on the exhale, causing your fingers to interlace.

2. Control

Increased stability and control are not only benefits of Pilates, they're also the objective. As you become more proficient, your ability to focus your mind and control individual muscles and muscle groups increases.

3. Concentration

Focusing on a given movement and being completely 'present' in the moment as you exercise is a skill you'll learn to hone through the workouts in this book. As a starting point, you'll need to pick a time and space for your workout that feels calm and free from distraction and interruption. Pilates isn't something you can do with the TV on in the background and dinner on the hob. Switch your phone to silent and retreat to the quietest room of your house when you know you can have at least 15 minutes to yourself. You shouldn't use music, as you'll need to be focused on the movements and, as you get more proficient, on your breath.

4. Precision

Quality, not quantity, is the ultimate rule in Pilates. Joseph Pilates' view was that it's far better to do three repetitions of an exercise correctly than 10 badly. He argued that when precision in movement is achieved, there's no need for lots of reps as the benefits of each single exercise are so powerful.

5. Breath

The most important thing of all in Pilates, particularly as a beginner, is to ensure you don't hold or restrict your breath. As you will be scooping your abdominals towards your spine, you'll need to breathe laterally (allowing your ribcage to expand out to the sides, so as not to arch in the back as you inhale and exhale). In the beginning do not put too much stress on the breath. Rather than holding it, breathe naturally.

As you become more proficient in the intermediate and advanced workouts, you can place more emphasis on co-ordinating your breath with your movements. As a general pointer, Pilates breath should be soft – you shouldn't hear it.

6. Flow

This is a principle that can only come with practice and experience, but ensuring your movements are as smooth and controlled as possible is a great starting point. Don't jerk from one position to another and aim to get a comfortable rhythm going as you get used to the sequence. Eventually, the whole sequence of exercises should become fluid, transitioning seamlessly from one exercise to another.

Left: Remembering the six principles of Pilates will help you to achieve perfect balance and control during the exercises.

Basic

These are the simplest, core Pilates exercises.
Practise this sequence regularly until you have
mastered all the exercises, and are able to fully
and confidently engage your powerhouse.

Perform the exercises in order, and stick to the number of repetitions recommended. For a handy illustrated reminder of the full sequence, consult the pull-out visual guide at the back of this book.

★ The hundred
★ Roll-up
★ Single leg circles
★ Rolling like a ball
★ Single leg stretch
★ Double leg stretch
★ Spine stretch forward

1 The hundred

▶▶▶ Working your powerhouse, this breathing exercise is a great warm-up, as it circulates oxygenated blood to all your muscles.

This exercise is good for engaging all the muscles in the powerhouse

★ BEST FOR WARMING UP

Pull your navel down towards the mat.

Keep your abs scooped while you pump your arms.

Pull your knees in towards your chest.

Keep your head and shoulders curled upwards

Pump your arms up and down

Zest tip
Maintain your abdominal scoop throughout and focus on breath control. Keep the pumps long and strong, pulling your shoulders away from your ears, neck long and relaxed.

If your lower back hurts, lift your leg higher or soften your knees. If your neck hurts, put it down for one inhale and exhale, then raise it back up once rested. Don't stop pumping.

PROGRESSION

Straighten your legs until they are at a 90-degree angle to the mat, inner thighs pressed together tightly.

Wrap your buttocks and draw your inner thighs together as you straighten your legs.

1 Begin by lying flat on your back, knees bent and arms alongside you.

2 Pull your knees in towards your chest and curl your head and shoulders upwards, eyes focused on your tummy, and chin over your chest, neck relaxed.

3 Raise your arms to hover above the mat, fingertips pointing forwards, and start to pump your arms up and down, keeping them straight and strong with your fingers long. Take care to keep the movement controlled; think of it as a vigorous patting motion. Breathe in for a count of 5, then out for 5 as you pump your arms. Do this 10 times. If you can keep your abdominals scooped while pumping, without arching your lower back, then try to straighten your legs towards the ceiling, wrapping your buttocks, drawing your inner thighs together, toes relaxed. Then lie back on your mat and hug your knees into your chest before placing your feet on the floor, knees bent, ready for the Roll-up.

PROGRESSION As you begin to feel stronger, and move on to the more advanced workouts, lower your legs straight to a 45-degree angle to the mat during this exercise, keeping your abdominals scooped and making sure your back doesn't begin to arch away from the mat (if it does, return your legs to the upright position). Continue to pump your arms, breathing for 100 counts.

2 Roll-up

▶▶▶ Works your abdominal scoop and strengthens and mobilises the spine.

BEST FOR A STRONG & FLEXIBLE BACK

Keep your chin tucked in.

Allow your head to lift up as you raise your arms.

Zest tip

Fluidity is the key to this exercise. Ensure you don't lurch (like a mummy coming out of a tomb!).

Keep your stomach scooped and maintain control as you roll forward.

Reach your hands forward to stretch as you roll up.

PROGRESSION

Look down into your navel to maintain the scoop

Scoop your stomach towards your spine.

1 Flat on your back, stretch out, with your arms above your head.

2 Bend your knees and place your feet together flat on the floor, then squeeze your buttocks together, imagining the muscles wrapping around your hips as you press your inner thighs together.

3 Lift your arms to a vertical stretch, straight up to the ceiling, and allow your head to come up too, inhaling as you start to roll forward and keeping your chin tucked in. If you need to, take hold of the backs of your thighs to make the roll-up smooth.

4 Continue to roll in a wave-like motion, pulling your chin towards your chest, your chest over your abs, and your abs over your pelvis. Keep going, reaching forward to stretch and exhaling, with your hands pointing towards your toes, at shoulder-height. Feel the two-way stretch. You should be reaching forward, with your tummy resisting and pulling back.

5 Now, reverse the exercise, beginning by inhaling as you scoop your stomach towards your spine, slightly tucking your pelvis under. Begin rolling down, vertebra by vertebra, drawing your inner thighs together as you roll to ensure you don't lose control.

6 Once your shoulders have contact with the mat, stretch your arms once again straight out either side of your head before repeating the sequence.

Do 3–5 repetitions, then roll back down to prepare for your Single Leg Circles.

PROGRESSION Once you can do this fluidly, without lurching, try it with your legs stretched out along the mat, feet in Pilates stance, buttocks wrapped.

3 Single leg circles

▶▶▶ Increases stability in your torso and mobility in your hip joint, and tapers your inner and outer thighs.

INTRODUCTION

INTERMEDIATE

ADVANCED

PILATES FOR YOU

BEST FOR
STABILITY IN
THE TORSO

Lengthen your neck and press your head into the mat.

Lead the circling movement with your inner thighs.

Stay anchored in your torso.

Keep your tailbone anchored.

PROGRESSION

Make sure you are stable in your torso, with your lower back rooted to the ground and your stationary leg and hip staying still.

Zest tip

As you circle, make sure that your active leg is relaxed in the hip joint. You want to ensure you maintain contact between your lower back and the mat and also take care to check your outer thighs aren't doing all the work.

Lengthen your stationary leg for an even greater challenge.

1 Lying on your back, extend your right leg towards the ceiling, left knee bent, foot on the mat, arms flat either side of your body with your tailbone anchored.

2 Once your leg is as close to 90 degrees as you can manage, lengthen your neck, pressing your head into the mat.

3 Stretch your right leg diagonally across your body, towards your left shoulder, then circle it down and back to its starting position, leading with your inner thighs.

4 Synchronise your breathing, inhaling as you begin each circle and exhaling as you finish. The most important thing in this exercise is to stay stable in the torso, to ensure your lower back is rooted to the ground and that your stationary leg and hip stay put. Try imagining your hips are bolted into the floor and press your arms and hands into the mat for extra stability.

Do 5 repetitions before reversing the direction of your leg for a further 5. Then switch legs and repeat the whole thing on the opposite side. Do a perfect roll-up then scoop your buttocks to the front of your mat ready for Rolling Like A Ball.

PROGRESSION If you can maintain your abdominal scoop while circling your leg, without any extra hip movement, then lengthen your opposing leg for an extra challenge.

Rolling like a ball

▶ ▶ ▶ Works deep into your abdominals, improves your balance, massages your spine.

INTRODUCTION

INTERMEDIATE

ADVANCED

PILATES FOR YOU

Zest tip

Don't throw your head back to initiate the rolling movement. Instead, keep your chin tucked in by looking into your navel, and use the power of your abdominal scoop to trigger the momentum.

BEST FOR
MASSAGING YOUR SPINE

Hug your ankles to your body.

Balance on your sitting bones.

Scoop your navel deep, drawing it towards your spine.

Roll back only as far as your shoulder blades.

Keep your chin tucked in and look towards your navel.

Keep your feet hovering above the mat and use your powerhouse to maintain your balance.

Squeeze your heels and buttocks to act as brakes. This will help you to maintain your balance.

INTRODUCTION

INTERMEDIATE

ADVANCED

PILATES FOR YOU

1 Sitting at the top of your mat, hug your ankles into your body and balance on your sitting bones.

2 Keep your heels together, feet off the mat, and drop your chin towards your knees so that you're looking into your navel. Your elbows should be bent out wide, like a beetle in its protective stance. Stay as tightly tucked as you can throughout the exercise.

3 Scoop your navel deep, drawing it towards your spine. This action should help you initiate a roll

backwards. Roll until you feel your shoulder blades on the mat, then roll back up again, like a rocking horse. Once back up, keep your feet hovering above the mat and use your powerhouse to maintain your balance.

Repeat this 5 or 6 times, inhaling as you roll back and exhaling as you come back up. On your final roll, finish by putting your heels down on the mat, and lifting your bottom up to move it backwards, away from your heels, to lie down ready for the Single Leg Stretch.

5 Single leg stretch

▶▶▶ First in the series of five major abdominal exercises: works the powerhouse, stretches your legs and enhances your co-ordination.

INTRODUCTION

BASIC

INTERMEDIATE

ADVANCED

PILATES FOR YOU

★

BEST FOR
STRENGTHENING
YOUR ABS

Extend your left leg up and out at a 45-degree angle to the mat.

★ Bad knee? Hold the underside of your thigh, pulling your leg into your chest. Keep your opposite leg high to the ceiling if your back begins to arch.

Curl up your head and shoulders.

Look towards your navel.

Stay anchored in your torso.

Switch arms and legs as you exhale.

Make sure your back is flat on the mat. If it begins to arch, lift your extended leg a little.

PROGRESSION

INTRODUCTION

BASIC

INTERMEDIATE

ADVANCED

PILATES FOR YOU

Zest tip

Mastering the co-ordination of this exercise takes practice. Don't rush! Remember to reach for your right ankle with your right hand, left ankle with your left hand.

As you progress with the exercise, try lowering your extended leg a little for an even greater challenge.

Keep your elbows wide and your shoulders down and relaxed.

1 Lie on your back, knees bent into your chest. Grab hold of your right ankle with your right hand and take your left hand on your right knee, extending your left leg up and out, at about 45 degrees to the floor, curling up your head and shoulders and looking toward your navel. Your elbows should be wide like, like a musician playing the saxophone, shoulders down and relaxed.

2 Check your back is flat on the mat and, if it begins to arch, lift your extended leg higher to the ceiling. This will ease the pressure on your lower back.

3 Exhale, switching legs and arms, so that your left knee is bent, with your left hand grasping your left ankle and right hand holding your left knee.

Repeat 5 times, then pull both legs into your chest to get ready for Double Leg Stretch.

PROGRESSION Try this with your extended leg stretched out long, to add an extra abdominal challenge.

▶▶▶ Second in the series of five major abdominal exercises: works your powerhouse and stretches out your entire body.

Look towards your navel.

Bend your elbows outwards.

Curl up your head and shoulders.

Stretch your arms up, so they are either side of your ears.

Don't lose your curl as the arms reach up.

PROGRESSION

As you progress with the exercise, try lowering your legs.

INTRODUCTION

INTERMEDIATE

ADVANCED

PILATES FOR YOU

Keep your chin over your chest to protect your neck.

Maintain your abdominal scoop.

Circle your arms out wide to the side as you exhale.

Zest tip

To work your deepest abdominals, try to keep your scoop when you extend out long and pull your navel further towards your spine as you exhale.

1 Lie on your back and pull both legs into your chest, curling up your head and shoulders, looking into your navel and grabbing your ankles, elbows bent outwards.

2 Inhale and lengthen your body, stretching your arms upwards, either side of your ears, legs out to the ceiling or at 45 degrees if you're stronger. Keep your back rooted to the mat and keep your chin over your chest to protect your neck.

3 Exhale, circling both arms out wide to the side, then keep exhaling as you pull your knees back into your chest.

Repeat 5 times, inhaling as you stretch out, and breathing out when you pull back to the start position, co-ordinating arms and legs so it becomes one smooth motion. Bend both knees into your chest and roll up to prepare for Spine Stretch Forward.

PROGRESSION Try this with your legs at 45 degrees to the mat to challenge your powerhouse more.

7 Spine stretch forward

▶▶▶ Works your deep abdominals, stretches and mobilises your spine, stretches your hamstrings, and empties your lungs.

INTRODUCTION

BASIC

INTERMEDIATE

ADVANCED

PILATES FOR YOU

Keep your arms at shoulder height, with your fingertips pointing forward.

Zest tip

Many people with tight hamstrings (particularly common if you run or cycle a lot) struggle to sit up straight. If you have this issue, try sitting on a cushion or softening your knees slightly. This is primarily a spine stretch. It's better to have a long flat back to start than to have stretched legs and look like a sack of potatoes!

Lift up off the buttocks with a perfectly straight back.

Flex your feet up to the ceiling.

Bend forward to create a C-shape with your spine. Your navel should be pulling in and you should feel a deep stretch in your back.

Force all the air out of your lungs as you bend forward.

1 Sit up tall on your mat, with your legs straight out in front of you, open slightly wider than hip-width.

2 Flex your feet up towards the ceiling. Straighten your arms out at shoulder height, fingertips pointing straight forward.

3 Inhale, lifting up even taller (aim to feel yourself growing 5cm/2 inches), then drop your chin towards your chest and round forward, hollowing out your abdominals and stretching your spine. Force all the air out of your lungs, feeling your core muscles engage.

4 Imagine you're making a letter C with your body, pulling your abdominal muscles in and up. You should feel a deep stretch in your back, but no pain.

5 Inhale, roll back up and sit tall.

Repeat this 3–5 times, deepening your stretch, without straining, with each repetition.

Intermediate

Once you feel comfortable and confident doing the basic sequence and can complete it smoothly, with one movement flowing into the next, breathing as the instructions recommend and keeping your powerhouse connected throughout, you're ready to move on to the next stage: the intermediate sequence.

Now that you're familiar with the basic sequence, the new exercises you will learn in this chapter can be slotted in at specific points to form the intermediate sequence listed below. Perform the exercises in order, and stick to the number of repetitions recommended. For a handy reference to the sequence order, consult the pull-out guide at the back of this book.

★ The hundred
★ Roll-up
★ Single leg circles
★ Rolling like a ball
★ Single leg stretch
★ Double leg stretch
★ Single straight leg stretch
★ Double straight leg stretch
★ Criss-cross
★ Spine stretch forward

★ Open leg rocker
★ Corkscrew
★ Saw
★ Neck roll
★ Single leg kicks
★ Double leg kicks
★ Neck pull
★ Side kick series
★ Teaser preparation
★ Teaser 1
★ Seal

Single straight leg stretch

▶▶▶ Third in the series of five major abdominal exercises: works the powerhouse and stretches the hamstrings deeply.

INTRODUCTION

BASIC

INTERMEDIATE

ADVANCED

PILATES FOR YOU

Tug your right leg towards you twice.

Extend your left leg out long. It should be hovering just above the mat.

BEST FOR
STRENGTHENING
YOUR ABS

Keep your chin tucked over your chest.

Lower your raised leg and raise your lower leg so that they pass like scissors.

Zest tip

If you can't hold your ankle, hold your calf. Try to keep your legs straight throughout. Pull your leg to your body, not your body to your leg. The pull should come from your tummy.

Tug your left leg towards you twice.

Your torso should remain stable and your powerhouse engaged.

1 On your back (following your Double Leg Stretch), knees in towards your chest and both elbows bent out to the sides, lift your head, chin tucked over your chest.

2 Inhale, raising your right leg directly up towards the ceiling and keeping hold of your right ankle with both hands, extending your left leg straight out long so it's hovering above the mat.

3 Exhale, sinking your spine into the mat beneath you and ensuring your torso remains stable and still, engaging your powerhouse.

4 Pull the raised leg towards you twice, keeping it super-straight, then switch legs in a scissor-like fashion.

5 Grasp the ankle of your left leg, and repeat the double tug, exhaling on each pull.

Do 5 reps, then finish with both legs raised up towards the ceiling.

▶▶▶ Fourth in the series of five major abdominal exercises: targets your lower abs as you use your powerhouse to raise and lower your legs.

Start with your feet in Pilates stance.

Keep your gaze focused on your stomach

BEST FOR
★
STRENGTHENING YOUR ABS

Squeeze your inner thighs and wrap your buttocks.

Squeeze your inner thighs even tighter as you lift your legs.

Use your lower abs to lower and lift your legs.

Zest tip

Only lower your legs as far as you can maintain your abdominal scoop. Small and precise is better than low with an arched back, however tempting this may be.

INTRODUCTION

BASIC

ADVANCED

PILATES FOR YOU

Keep your tailbone down on the mat as you lift your legs.

Lift your legs back up so that they are at a 90-degree angle to the mat.

Keep your upper back in its curl, perfectly still.

1 Take your hands behind your head (one on top of the other, rather than interlaced), keeping your legs up to the ceiling, feet in Pilates stance.

2 Squeeze your inner thighs together tightly, wrapping your buttocks.

3 Engage your powerhouse and lift your head, keeping your gaze focused on your stomach.

4 Slowly lower your legs back down towards the mat with control. Stop before you feel your lower back lose contact with the mat.

5 Squeeze your inner thighs tighter still and exhale as you draw your legs back up again, scooping them up using your abdominal strength. Make sure you keep your tailbone down, don't lift it off the mat.

Do 5 reps, then finish with both knees in to your chest.

▶▶▶ Fifth in the series of five major abdominal exercises: a fantastic waist trimmer and toner, this works your obliques.

Raise your head and place your hands behind it.

BEST FOR TESTING YOUR BALANCE

Your shoulders should stay above the mat.

Keep the lift in the upper back as you twist. Your hips should stay anchored.

Keep your torso anchored and try not to roll from side to side as you rotate.

Zest tip

Stay 'high' when you're transitioning from side to side: your shoulder blades should be just touching the mat.

1 Lie on your back, knees bent in towards your chest and raise your head, placing your hands behind your head.

2 Extend your left leg outwards in a long line in front of you, twisting your left elbow towards your right (bent) knee as you rotate your torso to the right.

3 Exhale, holding the position, feeling the stretch in your upper back and contraction in your transverse abdominals on your right side. Your shoulders should stay above the mat as you rotate, so you're supporting your body using your powerhouse, keeping your hips still.

4 Inhale and change sides, bringing your right elbow towards your left knee as you retract your left leg to bend it back in towards your chest, extending your right leg out in front of you.

5 Keep your midsection as rooted as possible, ensuring your hips stay anchored and avoiding rolling from side to side. The twist should occur at your ribs.

Do 5–10 reps before pulling your knees back into your chest, then straightening them out to roll up to a sitting position with control, ready for Spine Stretch Forward.

4 Open leg rocker

▶▶▶ Gives your spine a great massage, challenges your powerhouse to maintain your balance, and works your flexibility.

INTRODUCTION

BASIC

ADVANCED

PILATES FOR YOU

Grip your ankles from the inside. Your knees should be shoulder-width apart.

Keep your abdominals scooped towards your spine, your tailbone tucked under and your chest lifted.

Zest tip

Scoop your abdominals to trigger the rocking momentum back and also forwards.

Keep hold of your ankles as you straighten your legs. If you find this difficult then move your hands down a little to hold your calves.

Keep hold of your ankles or calves.

Make sure you keep your legs in position and keep your torso central.

Don't throw your head back to initiate the movement. Only roll as far as your shoulder blades.

Roll back as far as your shoulder blades.

INTRODUCTION

BASIC

INTERMEDIATE

ADVANCED

PILATES FOR YOU

1 Move to the front of your mat, bending your knees in towards your chest. Open your knees to shoulder-width, taking hold of your ankles from the inside. The photo shows the correct arm position.

2 Scoop your abdominals towards your spine, balancing in a C-curve, with your tailbone tucked underneath you and your chest lifted.

3 With control, straighten both legs out until your body resembles a V. If you can't keep hold of your ankles, hold your calves.

4 Inhale, scooping your abs towards your spine and tucking your chin into your chest. This action should trigger the rocking motion, sending you backwards.

5 Allow yourself to roll back, stopping when you feel the mat at the base of your shoulder blades, taking care to maintain your leg position, keeping your torso central.

6 Exhale, rolling back up and keeping your chin tucked in.

7 Once you find yourself back at your tipping point, stabilise yourself by pulling your tummy in further, taking care not to overbalance. Lift your chest.

Do 6 reps, then bring your legs together, lifting your arms up to the ceiling and lowering your body to the mat with control. Leave your legs up to the ceiling and bring your arms down flat by your sides.

5 Corkscrew

▶▶▶ Helps develop your balance and challenges the powerhouse.
It works your transverse abs while stretching your back.

*Scoop your stomach
towards your spine.*

Zest tip

Don't take any strain in your
neck or shoulders. Anchor
your shoulder blades down
into the mat, and keep your
head down flat, with your
neck long.

*Keep your inner thighs
tightly together and your
glutes wrapped.*

Zest tip

Hold your legs tightly
together. Make the
circles only as wide and
as low as you can.
Still keep your lower
back anchored to
the mat.

Reverse the direction of the circle, keeping your lower back firmly on the mat.

Try to keep the rest of your body completely still as you circle your legs.

INTRODUCTION

BASIC

INTERMEDIATE

ADVANCED

PILATES FOR YOU

1 Scoop your stomach towards your spine, draw your inner thighs tightly together, glutes wrapped.

2 Circle your legs to the right, down and back to the starting position, going clockwise.

3 Once you've completed one circle, reverse the direction, circling your legs to the left, down and back to the starting position, so they're going anticlockwise.

4 Keep going, reversing the direction of your circle with each rep, breathing in as you start the circle and exhaling as you complete it.

5 Make sure your lower back stays firmly on the mat as you move. Imagine your body is a deadweight and only your legs are able to move.

Do 3 each way, and finish by hugging your knees into your chest to stretch your lower back. Then, roll up to seated for Saw.

6 Saw

▶▶▶ A powerful breathing exercise which squeezes all the stale air out of your lungs, stretches the spine, hamstrings and targets your obliques.

INTRODUCTION

BASIC

INTERMEDIATE

ADVANCED

PILATES FOR YOU

Make sure your lats are pulling downward.

Squeeze your buttocks together and lift, to create exra length in the spine.

Keep your feet flexed, with your toes pointing upward.

BEST FOR TRIMMING YOUR WAIST

Lengthen your spine even further as you twist.

Your hips and buttocks should stay anchored.

Your head should be looking underneath your right armpit

Keep your right arm straight and extended behind you.

Pull your stomach in and up.

INTRODUCTION

BASIC

ADVANCED

PILATES FOR YOU

Zest tip

Think of the Saw as a Spine Stretch Forward with a twist. Use each twist to wring stale air out of your lungs, exhaling fully before inhaling.

1 Sit up in the middle of your mat, with your legs straight out in front, slightly wider than mat-width apart and feet flexed, toes pointing skyward.

2 Stretch both arms out horizontally, taking care to keep your lats pulling downwards, opening your upper back while keeping your ribcage down.

3 Inhale, lifting your stomach, so that your spine lengthens a few inches. Imagine your mat has suddenly got hot, so you lift yourself off it.

4 Twist your torso to the right, and get even taller, making sure that your hips and buttocks stay anchored. Exhale, reaching forwards with your left

arm, with your stomach pulling in and up, passing the little toe of your flexed right foot with your left hand, palms facing the mat. Your right arm should stay extended, reaching straight out behind you, creating a deep stretch in your chest as you hold the position with your head looking underneath your right armpit.

5 Inhale, keeping your powerhouse strong as you draw back to centre. Then twist to the left and 'saw off' your left little toe with your right hand.

Do 4 reps (alternating sides), then draw your legs together and flip on to your tummy ready for Neck Roll (Intermediate) or the Swan Dive (Advanced).

▶▶▶ Strengthens your upper back and stretches your neck.

INTRODUCTION

BASIC

ADVANCED

PILATES FOR YOU

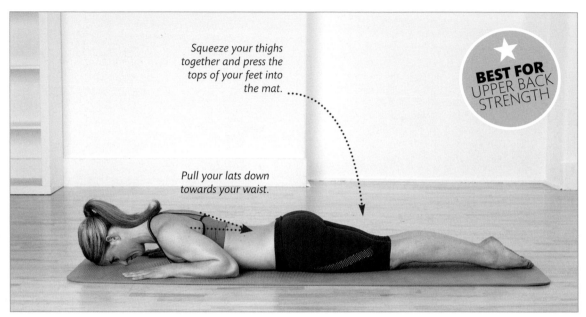

Squeeze your thighs together and press the tops of your feet into the mat.

BEST FOR
UPPER BACK
STRENGTH

Pull your lats down towards your waist.

Zest tip

Lift your chest only as high as you can while keeping your shoulders down. There should be no strain in the lower back.

Scoop your stomach towards your spine.

Lift your chest up off the mat.

Press your hands into the mat for support.

Zest tip
Keep your navel pulling in and glutes tight to protect your lower back

1 Lying on your stomach, palms pressing into the mat below your shoulders, squeeze your thighs together and press the tops of both feet into the mat.

2 Inhale, scooping your stomach towards your spine and pressing your hands into the mat, and start to lift your chest upwards, eyes staring straight ahead.

3 Turn your head to the left, then roll it down and over to your right, taking your chin to your chest midway, then rolling it back forward.

Repeat the Neck Roll, turning to the right side, then lower back down with control and repeat.

▶ ▶ ▶ Works your upper body as well as your buttocks and hamstrings, providing a great stretch in your thighs and hip flexors.

INTRODUCTION

BASIC

ADVANCED

PILATES FOR YOU

Press your fists into the mat, allowing your weight to rest on them.

Your shoulders and lats should be pulling down.

Squeeze your buttocks and thighs to support your back.

BEST FOR
TONING
YOUR BUM

Imagine your spine extending and lengthening through the back of your neck.

Zest tip
You shouldn't feel any pain at all in your lower back. Engaging your abs, inner thighs and glutes will protect you.

Lift your tummy up off the mat.

Pull your foot down towards your buttocks twice.

Switch legs and repeat the exercise

1 Bend your elbows directly under your shoulders, making fists with your hands, pressing them into the mat and resting your weight on them.

2 Scoop your stomach towards your spine, away from the mat, and squeeze your buttocks and thighs together to support your back.

3 Lift your upper back, pushing away from your elbows and forearms and thinking of opening and lifting your chest, imagining your spine extending and lengthening through the back of your neck.

4 Kick your left heel towards your left buttock with a double 'beat', then switch legs, extending your left leg back towards the mat, and lifting and beating your right heel.

5 Keep your abs scooped in and lifted throughout.

Do 5 reps, alternating legs (right and left is 1 rep). Lower your body back down until you're flat on the mat, face to the left, ready for Double Leg Kicks.

9 Double leg kicks

▶▶▶ Works the entire back of your legs and buttocks, as well as giving a deep shoulder and upper back stretch.

INTRODUCTION

BASIC

ADVANCED

PILATES FOR YOU

Clasp your hands as high up your back as you can without lifting your elbows or shoulders off the mat.

★ **BEST FOR** OPENING YOUR CHEST

Fan your elbows down to the mat to create a nice opening in the upper back

Kick your heels towards your bottom three times.

Press your pubic bone down into the mat as the heels pull in towards the bottom. Make sure your bottom doesn't lift up.

Squeeze your shoulder blades together and downwards.

Reach your arms down your back as you lower your heels.

Zest tip

Don't lift your feet off the mat. Keep them glued down and make sure you're working your upper, not your lower, back.

Scoop your stomach in towards your spine.

1 On your stomach, with your face resting to the left, clasp your hands behind your back, as high as is possible, while still keeping the fronts of your shoulders and your elbows in contact with the mat.

2 Squeeze your buttocks and thighs together, engaging your powerhouse as you kick both heels towards your bottom, pulsing three times, like a mermaid's tail.

3 With control, move both your legs back down the mat and reach your arms back to follow them, keeping them clasped, drawing your upper back upwards and scooping your stomach in towards your spine as you do. Your nose should be facing forwards.

4 Hold this position, deepening the stretch and reach of your arms, squeezing your shoulder blades together and downwards, keeping your neck long. Press your legs and feet into the mat for stability as you stretch.

5 Lower your upper body to the mat, resting your head to the right, bringing your hands back to their initial clasped position under the shoulder blades and bending your legs once more.

Do a further 3 sets of the three-pulse kicks, then release your lower back by sitting back onto your heels in Child's Pose (see page 21).

▶ ▶ ▶ Strengthens your powerhouse and stretches your upper back and neck.

INTRODUCTION

BASIC

ADVANCED

PILATES FOR YOU

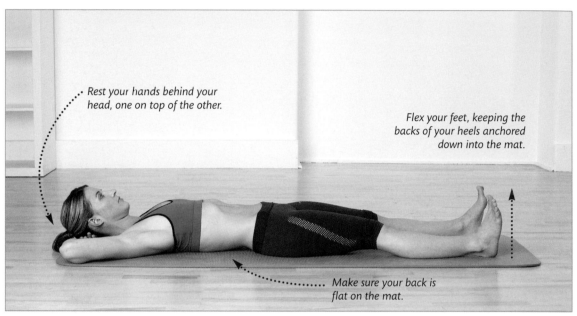

Rest your hands behind your head, one on top of the other.

Flex your feet, keeping the backs of your heels anchored down into the mat.

Make sure your back is flat on the mat.

Try to keep your elbows wide as you roll up to challenge your powerhouse.

Keep your legs still as you roll up.

Scoop your stomach.

Your head should be looking down between your knees.

Bend forward to create a C-shape with your spine.

Zest tip

Give each vertebra a chance to peel up from the mat, bit by bit, and imprint bone by bone back down on the mat. This is not an easy exercise to keep fluid now that your arms are restricted behind your head.

Keep your elbows as wide as possible.

1 Lie on your back, resting your hands one underneath the other, behind your head. Your legs should be extended straight out, slightly wider than hip-width apart, with the backs of your heels anchored into your mat, feet flexed.

2 Scoop your stomach towards your spine and check your back is flat.

3 Inhale, slowly rolling up and forward, keeping your elbows out wide and glutes engaged. As with the Roll-up (see page 28), repeat the sensation of curling in on yourself, stretching your chin to chest and aiming to take your ribs over your tummy and tummy over your hips, keeping your legs still.

4 Exhale, rounding your torso forward so that your head is staring at the mat between your knees.

5 Inhale, returning to an upright position with control, elbows wide.

6 Exhale and, tucking your pelvis under slightly, slowly roll your spine back down to the mat. Keep your navel pulled in so that the roll is smooth and controlled, pressing your head back into your hands to give the neck stretch.

Do 5 reps.

Side kick series

INTRODUCTION

BASIC

INTERMEDIATE

ADVANCED

PILATES FOR YOU

►►► This whole intermediate side kick series works the waist, hips, buttocks and thighs. These exercises are great for sculpting leaner legs and testing your balance and control.

Zest tip

Throughout the side kick series, keep your navel pulling in and away from your left elbow and your shoulder blades pulling down towards your waist to lengthen your neck. To maintain stability, imagine you have a pint of water balancing on your upper shoulder.

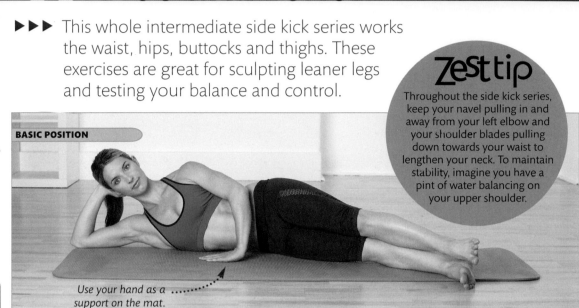

BASIC POSITION

Use your hand as a support on the mat.

PROGRESSION

Hold your hand behind your head in the advanced side kick series to further test your balance.

1 Lie on your right side, in one long line, then move your legs forward to a 45-degree angle to your body, feet in Pilates stance (maintaining a slightly rotated hip works your inner thighs and bottom more effectively). Bend your right arm, resting your hand on the side of your head. Place your left hand in front of your belly button, flat on the mat for support. Keep your upper body as stable as possible, ensuring you don't roll back and forth.

PROGRESSION Challenge yourself and take your top arm behind your head to test your stability and control.

►►► Forward and back

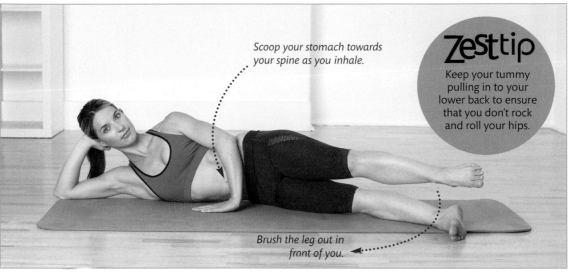

Scoop your stomach towards your spine as you inhale.

Zesttip
Keep your tummy pulling in to your lower back to ensure that you don't rock and roll your hips.

Brush the leg out in front of you.

Maintain the stablility in your hips and torso.

Pulse the leg forward twice before sweeping it to the back.

1 From your basic side kick series position, lift your top leg a little, turning your hip out slightly.

2 Inhale, scooping your stomach towards your spine, and brush your leg forward, out in front of you, pulsing it twice as far as it will go while still maintaining the stability in your hips and torso.

3 Exhale, smoothly sweeping your leg back behind you, as far as it will stretch without causing your body to rock and your back to arch.

Do 5 reps.

▶▶▶ Up and down

INTRODUCTION

BASIC

ADVANCED

PILATES FOR YOU

Turn your upper leg out slightly at the hip.

BEST FOR
TONING
YOUR
THIGHS

Lift your leg as close to vertical as you can without folding your torso inwards.

Keep your torso stable as you lift your leg.

Zest tip

Imagine you're reaching your upper leg as far away from you as possible as you lower it down.

Squeeze your inner thighs together and wrap your buttocks. ......

Use your inner thighs and buttocks to lower the leg back down to just above your stationary leg.

1 From your basic side kick series position, with your upper leg slightly turned out at the hip, inhale and lift your upper leg straight up to the ceiling (or as close to vertical as you can without folding your torso inwards).

2 Pause, then exhale as you stretch it back down with your foot flexed, imagining the leg coming to rest just above your lower leg, but 5cm (2in) longer than it was before, squeezing your inner thighs together and wrapping your buttocks.

3 Throughout the exercise, use your powerhouse to do the work and ensure your torso stays stable, like concrete. Use your inner thighs and buttocks to lift and lower the leg.

Do 5 reps slowly.

Side kick series

▶ ▶ ▶ Small circles

Zest tip
Find yourself wobbling?
Pull your stomach
towards your spine.
Lengthen through
your neck and imagine
yourself growing
longer.

BEST FOR
TONING
YOUR BUM
AND THIGHS

Squeeze your bottom
and inner thighs as
you circle.

Circle your heel forwards
in a vigorous rhythm, but
keep the circles small
and controlled.

INTRODUCTION

BASIC

INTERMEDIATE

ADVANCED

PILATES FOR YOU

You should feel your upper thighs working.

Keep the working leg slightly turned out to wrap the buttocks and target the inner thighs more effectively.

1 From your basic side series position, lift your top heel slightly and perform small circles forwards around your ankle, drawing an imaginary circle with your toe, keeping a vigorous rhythm, but ensuring your circles are small and controlled. Squeeze your bottom and inner thighs as you circle. You should feel your upper thighs working.

2 Do 5 reps, then reverse the movement for a further 5.

3 Roll over onto your tummy, forehead on your hands, elbows wide and perform Beating Your Legs (see page 120 for how to do this transition exercise) before repeating the whole side kick series on your other side. Once you've completed your final circle on your second side, roll over onto your back, knees bent, ready for Teaser Preparation.

▶▶▶ A preparation for the full Teaser exercise, this challenges your powerhouse and helps you to keep your lower body still. It will help you build the necessary strength and control before you move on.

INTRODUCTION

BASIC

ADVANCED

PILATES FOR YOU

Straighten your leg until it is at a 45-degree angle to the mat, keeping your knees together.

Reach your arms forward and follow them up with your chest.

Scoop your stomach towards your spine.

The roll-up should be smooth and controlled. Don't lurch upwards.

Pause in this position for a count of three.

Zesttip

Imagine your knees are super-glued together and keep your stomach scooped.

1 Begin on your back, with your knees bent, feet flat on the mat, and arms stretched out behind you, either side of your ears. Straighten your right leg to 45 degrees, keeping your knees together.

2 Scoop your stomach towards your spine and roll up, reaching your arms forward to your toe and following them by lifting your chest until your torso is slightly more than 45 degrees to the mat.

3 Pause for a count of 3, then lift the arms and chest up before lowering down with control, stretching your arms back behind you again.

4 Keep your knee where it is, and roll up again twice more, before repeating on the other side.

5 If you can perform this Preparation with strength and control, try Teaser 1.

6 End by pulling your knees into your chest to release your back, then return your legs to the ceiling if you're ready for Teaser 1, or if not, move to sit at the front of your mat, ready for Seal.

13 Teaser 1

▶▶▶ Really tests the strength of your powerhouse.

Lower your legs until they are at a 45-degree angle to the mat.

Scoop your stomach towards your spine.

Keep your lower back on the mat.

Zest tip
Roll up smoothly, reaching for your toes and controlling your centre on the way down.

Reach your hands towards your feet as you bring up your chest.

Reach for your toes.

Balance on your tailbones.

Reach up to the ceiling, opening your chest.

Leave your legs behind as you roll back down.

1 Lying on your back, feet raised to the ceiling in Pilates stance, stretch your arms over your head, alongside your ears. Lower your legs to 45 degrees, scooping your stomach towards your spine and inhale as you draw your arms forward, reaching for your feet. Your upper body should follow your arms, chest leading, until you're in a V position, balancing on your tailbone, with your arms parallel to your legs.

2 Lift up to the ceiling with your arms, then leave your legs behind, exhale rolling slowly back down on the mat and stretching your arms back out overhead before repeating.

Do 3 reps. Then either stay up in your V position ready for Teaser 2 in the advanced sequence or roll back down and hug your knees to your chest, before moving to the front of the mat, ready for Seal.

▶▶▶ Gives your back a fantastic massage and helps with balance and co-ordination.

Pull your feet up off the mat, with the soles together.

Keep your abs pulling into your lower back to create a round spine and aid the roll.

Keep your pelvis tucked underneath.

Clap the soles of your feet together 3 times.

Bad neck? Take care not to roll too far back or pass on this exercise altogether.

Maintain your shape as you roll backwards.

Make sure you are not resting on your neck when you roll backwards.

Zesttip

Make sure you engage your powerhouse to stay still whenever you're clapping. This will test your balance. Enjoy it – find the childlike rhythm of it and indulge your playful side!

Stop rolling forwards once you are balancing on your tailbone again.

Clap the soles of your feet together 3 times.

1 Sit at the front of your mat, knees bent, and feed your hands through the middle of your legs, sliding a hand around the back of each corresponding foot. Pull your feet up off the mat, keeping your soles together and balancing on the base of your spine, pelvis tucked underneath.

2 Inhale, scooping your stomach towards your spine, and roll back, maintaining your shape, like a ball.

3 Continue rolling until you're balancing on your shoulder blades and ensuring you're not resting on your neck.

4 Clap your soles together three times (like a seal flapping its flippers!), then exhale, rolling forward smoothly and stopping when you're balancing on your tailbone once more, then clap your soles together 3 more times, maintaining your balance in this position, before rolling back again.

Do 6 reps, aiming not to overbalance at either end of your 'rock,' and keeping your powerhouse activated throughout.

Advanced

▶ ▶ ▶ Once you feel comfortable and confident doing the intermediate sequence and can complete it smoothly, with one movement flowing into the next, breathing as the instructions recommend and keeping your powerhouse connected throughout, you're ready to increase your Pilates repertoire and move on to the next stage: the advanced sequence.

Now that you're familiar with the intermediate sequence, the new exercises you will learn in this chapter can be slotted in at specific points to form the advanced sequence listed below. Perform the exercises in order, and stick to the number of repetitions recommended. For a handy reference to the sequence order, consult the pull-out guide at the back of this book.

★ The hundred
★ Roll-up
★ Roll-over
★ Single leg circles
★ Rolling like a ball
★ Single leg stretch
★ Double leg stretch
★ Single straight leg stretch

★ Double straight leg stretch
★ Criss-cross
★ Spine stretch forward
★ Open leg rocker
★ Full corkscrew
★ Saw
★ Swan dive
★ Single leg kicks
★ Double leg kicks
★ Neck pull
★ Shoulder bridge
★ Spine twist
★ Jackknife
★ Side kick series
★ Teaser 1
★ Teaser 2
★ Teaser 3

★ Hip circles
★ Swimming
★ Leg pull down
★ Leg pull-up
★ Kneeling side kicks
★ Mermaid side stretch
★ Boomerang
★ Seal
★ Push-ups

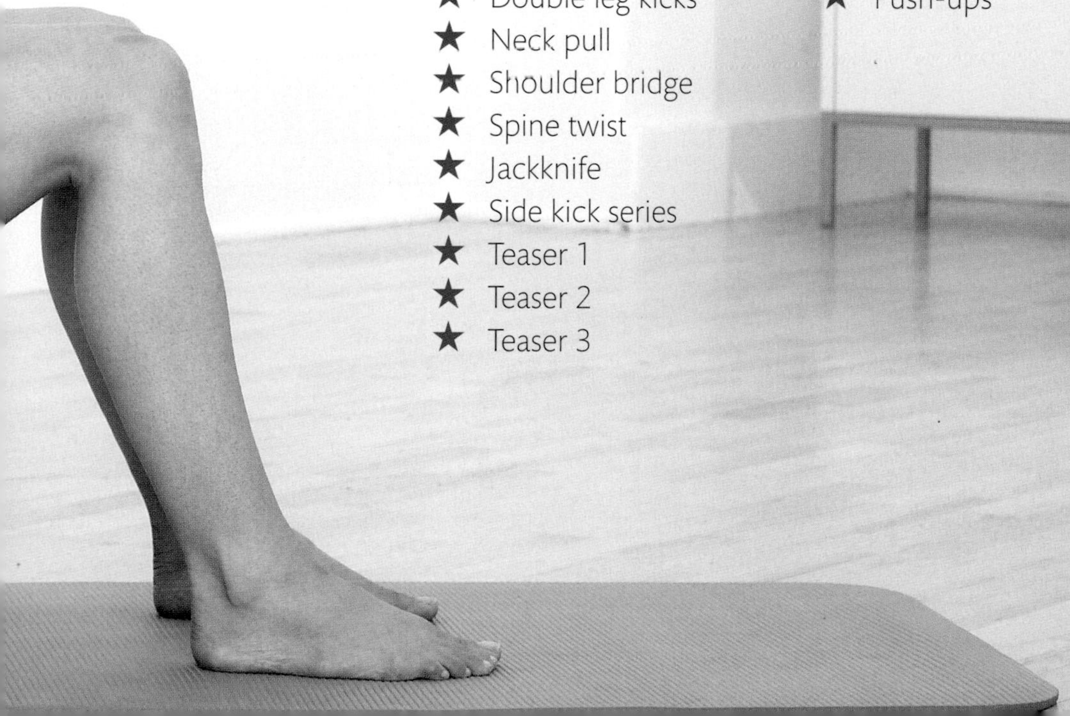

Roll-over

▶▶▶ The Roll-over follows the Roll-up, stretching and mobilising your spine, and further challenging your powerhouse.

INTRODUCTION

BASIC

INTERMEDIATE

ADVANCED

PILATES FOR YOU

Engage your abdominals and pull your lower back down to the mat.

lift your legs up over your head.

Press your arms into the mat to stabilise yourself.

Zest tip

Don't jerk up and over. This is only your third exercise, so take care to keep the motion smooth and controlled, lifting your legs from your powerhouse.

Make sure you don't roll onto the back of your neck.

Separate your feet hip-width apart.

Roll your spine slowly back down onto the mat, one vertebra at a time.

Use your arms to help you control the movement.

Roll through your spine and then lower your legs until they are at a 45-degree angle to the mat before bringing them together.

1 Lying on the mat, arms long by your sides, palms facing into the mat, wrap your buttocks and inhale as you scoop your stomach towards your spine, using your powerhouse to lift your legs off the mat and up over your head and beyond, until they're parallel to the mat.

2 Take care not to roll onto the back of your neck, pressing into your shoulder blades and, using your arms to stabilise you, pressing into the mat.

3 Open your legs to hip-width, exhaling as you roll your spine back down towards the mat with control, taking time to feel each vertebra imprint

as you go. Use your arms to keep the movement slow and controlled.

4 Once your buttocks touch down, keep lowering your legs until you reach the point where your spine is about to arch away from the mat. Then squeeze your legs together and repeat the motion.

5 Do 3 reps with your legs closed on the way up and open on the way down, then reverse to do 3 reps with your legs open on the way up, closed on the way down. Finish flat on the mat, arms long, ready for Single Leg Circles.

►►► Takes the abdominal workout and balance challenge of the Corkscrew to a more advanced level, intensifying the stretch of your back muscles.

★ BEST FOR
STRENGTHENING
YOUR ABS

Zest tip

Squeeze your buttocks and thighs together throughout to keep your lower back protected. All control should come from your abdominals and the pressure from the backs of your arms pressing into your mat.

Keep your torso stable as you circle your legs.

Lift your hips by squeezing your buttocks to balance vertically in a shoulder-stand.

Press your arms into the mat for stablility.

1 From your Open Leg Rocker position, bring your legs together, lift your arms up to the ceiling and, with control, slowly lower your body to the mat, leaving your legs raised and lowering your arms to rest by your sides, pressing into the mat.

2 Keeping both legs together, circle them round to the right. Keep your torso stable as you do this, completing a large rotation.

3 Pushing both arms into the mat for stability, lift your hips up and raise your legs up to the ceiling to balance in a shoulder stand.

4 Lower your legs slightly over your head and, from this position, roll down on the left side of your spine, circling your legs round to the left. Then lift back up onto your shoulders.

5 Do 3 on each side, alternating each time, then, from your last shoulder-stand, roll through the spine before lowering your legs down to the mat with control. Then roll up to a sitting position, legs extended and open slightly wider than mat-width, ready for Saw.

3 Swan dive

▶▶▶ Stretches and strengthens your back, neck and shoulders.

Keep your shoulders down as you rise up from the mat.

Keep your inner thighs together. Press your hips, thighs and tops of your feet into the mat.

Make sure your lats are pulling down towards your waist.

Lift up your tummy from the mat.

Rock forwards onto your breastbone.

Your body should be the shape of the base of a rocking horse or chair.

Keep your limbs straight and your powerhouse engaged as you rock back up.

Zest tip
To create the ideal lift, imagine you're throwing up a ball as you rock backwards. Take care to keep the back of your neck long.

1 On your stomach, elbows bent, palms sinking into the mat beneath your shoulders, with your hips, thighs and tops of your feet pressing into your mat. Inhale, scooping your navel towards your spine.

2 Press away from the mat, lifting your upper body and keeping your shoulders down. Your head and neck should be long and free, an extension of your spine.

3 Bend your arms once more as you lower down to the mat. Ensure that you keep wrapping your buttocks and keep your thighs zipped together to protect your back.

4 Repeat 3 times as a warm-up for the rest of the exercise.

5 On your fourth stretch upward, when you're in the lifted position, chest reaching toward the ceiling, release your hands out in front of you and rock forward, lifting your legs up behind you as you roll onto your breastbone (so your body looks like the base of a rocking chair).

6 Use the momentum to rock back up again, exhaling and keeping your limbs straight and your powerhouse engaged.

Do 3–5 repetitions, then sit back on your heels, head to the mat, in Child's Pose (see page 21), before lying down on your stomach, ready for Single Leg Kicks.

4 Shoulder bridge

▶▶▶ Strengthens the hamstrings and buttocks.

Lift up your buttocks and pull your navel in.

Tuck your thumbs in towards your sacrum and hug your hips with your fingers.

Zesttip

Ground the heel of your stabilising leg into the mat to strengthen your glutes and hamstrings while the opposite leg is moving.

Flex your foot and then lower your leg.

Scoop your stomach in towards your spine.

BEST FOR TONING YOUR BUM

When it's almost touching the mat, point your foot and lift it back up.

1 Lying on the mat, bend your knees, keeping your legs hip-width apart, feet flat on the floor pointing forward.

2 Squeeze your bottom as you roll your pelvis up, sliding your hands under your lower back and tucking your thumbs in towards your sacrum, fingers hugging your hips as you rest on your elbows.

3 Scoop your stomach in towards your spine, engaging your powerhouse, then stretch your

right leg directly in front of you, before swinging it up to the ceiling with your toes pointed, breathing in as you go.

4 Once your foot reaches the top, flex it, stretching your hamstring and calf to lengthen it away, before exhaling and lowering your foot back down to almost touch the mat, then lift back up. Do 3 reps on each side, lengthening out of the hip every time you lower. Then roll the pelvis down with control, then roll up to sitting, extending your legs out forward along the mat, ready for Spine Twist.

5 Spine twist

▶▶▶ A breathing exercise that expels stale air from your body and stretches the spine and surrounding muscles, working the waist.

BEST FOR TRIMMING YOUR WAIST

Lift up through the top of your head to lengthen your spine.

Your legs should be firmly 'stuck' together.

Keep your shoulders and arms level.

Empty the last bits of air out of your lungs as you twist further to the right.

The twist should occur at your navel.

Zest tip

Keep the length in your back as you twist, getting longer not shorter. Maintain the flexed stretch in your heels and make sure not to shorten one leg as you twist. Keep them both of equal length throughout.

Keep your heels and arms level to the mat.

1 Sit up tall in the middle of your mat, legs 'stuck' together out in front of you, feet together and flexed and arms lifted out to either side, palms facing the floor.

2 Inhale and lift up tall, then exhale, twisting your trunk to the right, then increasing the twist as you squeeze the last bits of air out of your lungs. Increase the length in your spine, and keep your shoulders pulled down as you squeeze your legs together. Keep both your arms and your heels level with the mat.

3 Empty your lungs, before inhaling and returning to centre.

4 Repeat the twist to the left. Do 3 reps on each side, alternating each time, before returning to centre and lying down flat on your back, ready for the Jackknife.

6 Jackknife

▶▶▶ A great strengthener for your powerhouse and your arms. It also stretches your neck and shoulders.

INTRODUCTION

BASIC

INTERMEDIATE

ADVANCED

PILATES FOR YOU

Don't attempt this if you've got a bad back or neck.

Scoop your tummy to lift your legs off the mat.

Squeeze your buttocks and thighs together.

Stop the movement when you are resting on your shoulder blades.

Zest tip
Imagine you're an Olympic diver in motion as your legs perform the jackknife dive.

Your legs should be parallel to the mat.

Press your arms into the mat for stability.

Push your hips upward, straighten your legs and point your toes.

Use your abdominal strength and control to keep your legs from flopping over your head on the roll down.

1 Lie flat on your back on your mat, hands palm-down by your sides and feet relaxed in Pilates stance.

2 Inhale, scooping your stomach towards your spine, as you squeeze your buttocks and thighs together tightly, lifting your legs off the mat and pulling them over your head, lifting your hips by squeezing your buttocks and using your powerhouse to support the movement. Stop when you're resting on your shoulder blades, keeping your feet tracking straight out behind your head and your legs are parallel to the mat.

3 Pause, then press your arms into the mat for stability, lifting up to a shoulder-stand position, pushing your hips upward, legs vertical and toes pointed.

4 From this position, exhale, rolling back down vertebra by vertebra, taking care to keep your toes over your nose. Aim to keep your hips and legs in the air until the last moment, resisting the urge to flop them back down over your head.

5 Once your back is flat on the mat, lengthen your legs towards the floor, without touching the mat, then repeat the whole movement.

Do 3 reps, then bring your knees in to your chest to release your lower back and roll onto your right side, ready for the Side Kick Series.

Side kick series: advanced

▶ ▶ ▶ **Grand rond de jambe** Encourages mobility in the hip joint, and stretches the hip flexors, working the powerhouse by testing your balance.

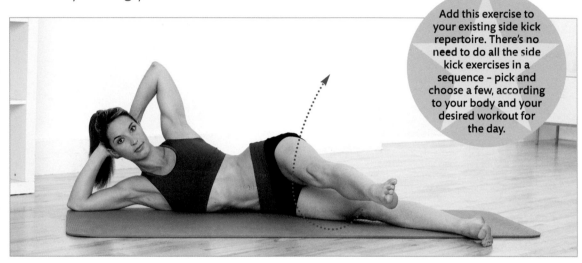

Add this exercise to your existing side kick repertoire. There's no need to do all the side kick exercises in a sequence – pick and choose a few, according to your body and your desired workout for the day.

Keep your tummy pulled in, your hips forward and your back long to counter the stretch.

Brush your leg forwards and then up to the ceiling before extending it behind you, as though you are painting a big circle in the air.

Zesttip

Be careful not to sink in your middle or collapse into your shoulders. Keep your spine lengthened and don't let those hips roll!

Repeat the circle three times and then reverse the movement.

Don't allow your back to arch.

1 From your advanced sidekick position (see the progression on page 62), inhale and sweep your leg out to the front, circling it to the ceiling, then back out behind you, drawing a big circle in the air.

Do 3 reps in each direction.

2 Ensure you counter the stretch in your back by keeping your tummy pulled in, hips firm and forward, and back long, stretching the full length of your spine and taking care not to let your back arch.

3 Repeat the sequence with control 3 times, before reversing the movement.

Side kick series: advanced

INTRODUCTION

BASIC

INTERMEDIATE

ADVANCED

PILATES FOR YOU

►►► **Inner thigh circles and lifts** Works your inner and outer thighs.

Pull your shoulder down to lengthen your neck.

Lift and lower your extended leg. Make sure it doesn't touch the mat.

Circle forwards five times and then backwards five times.

Zest tip
Keep your out-stretched leg long, extending out through the heel. Use your inner thigh to make the movement.

1 Lie on your right side, right elbow bent, hand supporting your head, left knee bent, resting your foot on the mat in front of you. Stretch your left arm long to grab your left ankle from the inside, pulling your left shoulder down.

2 Extend your right leg, freeing it from your hip joint, and rotate your heel slightly upward towards the ceiling, scooping your stomach towards your spine.

3 Lift and lower your leg with control, ensuring it doesn't touch the mat. Do this 5 times, then hold it in its upward position, pulsing it up a little further for 10 counts.

4 From this position, try 5 circles backwards and 5 circles forwards.

5 Slide your left leg back down to rest on top of your right leg. Stretch both legs out long for Double Leg Lifts.

► ► ► **Double leg lifts** Works your whole powerhouse and your transverse abdominals, in particular, toning the waist.

INTRODUCTION

BASIC

INTERMEDIATE

ADVANCED

PILATES FOR YOU

Your legs should be at a 45-degrees angle to the rest of your body.

Zest tip

Don't kick your legs behind your body line, arching your back in an effort to lift them higher. Keep your stomach strong, using your abdominal scoop to lift your legs.

Squeeze your thighs together and wrap your buttocks.

Use your transverse abdominals to lift and lower your legs.

1 In the advanced side kick position (see page 62), take your legs 45 degrees forward from your body Squeeze both thighs together, wrapping your buttocks, feet in Pilates stance. Use your waist (your transverse abdominals) to lift both legs up off the mat together. Then lower them back down.

Do 5–10 reps.

▶ ▶ ▶ **Bicycles** Works your powerhouse, challenging your hips, glutes and transverse abdominals.

INTRODUCTION

BASIC

INTERMEDIATE

ADVANCED

PILATES FOR YOU

Extend the leg back to start pedalling forwards.

Keep your torso stable and your waist long.

Zest tip

Keep your top leg at hip level, especially as your leg cycles out in front or extends to the back. Aim to get your heel as close to your buttock as possible when you bend your leg, pressing your knee back to get the best hip flexor stretch.

Increase the bend in your leg before extending your foot forward.

1 From your advanced side kick position (see the progression on page 62), brush your top leg forward and imagine your foot is resting on the pedal of a bicycle. Cycle forward 3 times, keeping your torso stable and your waist long.

2 Pause, then cycle backwards 3 times, before returning to your advanced side kick position.

3 Roll onto your tummy to do your transition Beating Your Legs or Frog Lifts (see pages 120–21),

then repeat the whole side kick series with the other leg.

4 On the final rep on your second side, roll over to your back, both feet to the ceiling, feet in Pilates stance, and prepare for Teaser 1.

▶▶▶ Improves balance and co-ordination and works your powerhouse.

INTRODUCTION

BASIC

INTERMEDIATE

ADVANCED

PILATES FOR YOU

BEST FOR STRENGTHENING YOUR ABS

Balance on your tailbone and scoop your stomach towards your spine.

Zesttip

Imagine your upper body is 'frozen' in position as you move your legs. Watch out for your shoulders starting to raise up in an effort to lift your legs.

Lower both legs slowly, without moving your torso.

Keep your torso still as you lower your legs.

Use your abdominal strength, not your thighs, to hold up your legs. . .

Exhale and lift your legs back up again.

1 From your Teaser 1 position (see pages 70–71), balancing on your tailbone, with your stomach scooped in towards your spine, hold your torso still and inhale as you lower both legs with control towards the mat.

2 Don't let your legs touch down. Instead aim to get them within a few inches of the mat before you exhale, using the strength of your powerhouse to lift them back up again. Use your tummy, not your thighs, to do the lifting.

Do 2–3 reps. Finish your last rep in the Teaser position once more, ready for Teaser 3.

9 Teaser 3

▶▶▶ Combines the actions of Teaser 1 and 2, using your whole body.

INTRODUCTION

BASIC

INTERMEDIATE

ADVANCED

PILATES FOR YOU

Balance on your tailbone and scoop your stomach towards your spine.

Keep your shoulders down and your neck long.

Lift up your arms and your chest before rolling down.

Zest tip

Imprint each of your vertebrae onto the mat as you roll down and peel each one off the mat on your way back up. Try not to leave any out!

Keep your stomach scooped.

Feel each vertebra imprint onto the mat as you roll down.

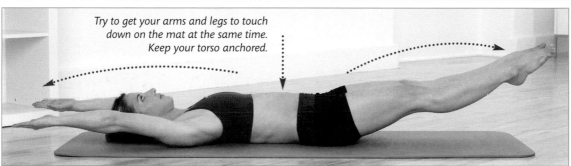

Try to get your arms and legs to touch down on the mat at the same time. Keep your torso anchored.

1 Already in your Teaser 1 position (see pages 70–71), balancing on your tailbone, keep your powerhouse engaged.

2 Raise your arms directly up to the ceiling alongside your ears, keeping your shoulders down and your neck long. Then, with control, roll your entire body and legs back down towards the mat, keeping your stomach scooped, and trying to feel each vertebra as it comes down, keeping the space and length between them.

Your arms should reach straight overhead to the wall behind you, legs out long.

3 Try to get both your arms and legs to touch down simultaneously, then fold straight back up into your Teaser 1 position. Initiate each roll down and roll back up by scooping your navel towards your spine.

Do 3 reps and on your last one stay up, extending your arms behind you to the mat, ready for your Hip Circles.

▶▶▶ Stretches your shoulders and chest and works the powerhouse.

Circle your legs round to the right.

This is a great stretch for the front of your shoulders, but if you have a weakness or injury in this area, it's best to leave it out.

Your ribs should be held in and not pushing out.

Zest tip

Keep lifting and stretching your chest up and outward, away from your arms, ensuring your back stays straight so that you don't 'sink' with the weight of your lifted legs.

Keep your palms pressing into the mat.

INTRODUCTION

BASIC

INTERMEDIATE

ADVANCED

PILATES FOR YOU

Keep your trunk stable and still.

Repeat the circle to the left. Use your inner thighs and lower abdominals to make the movement.

Zest tip

Stability is key here, so try to imagine your trunk is frozen in place, hands deeply rooted into the floor.

1 Begin balancing on your tailbone, with your legs held in the Teaser position, feet in Pilates stance and your arms straight out behind you, fingers pointing backwards and palms pressing into the mat.

2 Check that your ribs are held in and not pushing out, and inhale, keeping your feet in Pilates stance, circling your legs to the right, clockwise, inhaling as you start the circle and exhaling as you complete it. Then reverse the motion to complete an anticlockwise circle.

3 With each circle, change direction and maintain the rhythm of breath, ensuring that you're using the lower abdominals and inner thighs, rather than the quads.

Do 3 reps (a rep is 1 circle in each direction), before lowering your legs back down to the mat with control. Roll over for Swimming.

▶▶▶ A great workout for all your back muscles and a breathing exercise.

INTRODUCTION

BASIC

INTERMEDIATE

ADVANCED

PILATES FOR YOU

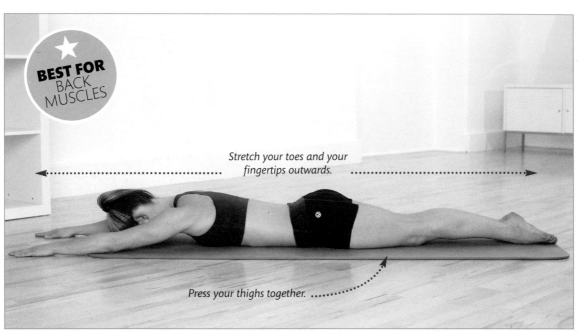

BEST FOR
BACK
MUSCLES

Stretch your toes and your fingertips outwards.

Press your thighs together.

Raise your head and chest off the floor.

Scoop your stomach towards your spine.

Zest tip

Keep your stomach tight. Aim to feel as if you're being stretched from your fingers to your toes, keeping your neck long.

Keep the kicking of your arms and legs vigorous. This will pump fresh blood and oxygen through your body, and test the stability of your trunk.

1 Lie face down on your mat, arms and legs completely outstretched with your thighs pressing together, feet in Pilates stance. Stretch your fingertips to the wall in front of you and your toes to the wall behind you.

2 Inhale, scooping your stomach towards your spine, and lift your right arm and left leg up off the mat simultaneously with control, holding them in position as you raise your head and chest off the mat.

3 Switch sides, lowering the raised limbs and swapping for the other side. Now continue the kicking motion, at a faster pace, imagining that there's a shark behind you! Maintain a steady breathing rhythm throughout, inhaling for 5 counts, and exhaling for 5 counts (like your Hundreds; see page 26).

Do 3 sets, then sit back on your heels to release your lower back in Child's Pose (see page 21).

12 Leg pull down

▶▶▶ Stretches your Achilles tendons and calves and tests the stability of your powerhouse.

INTRODUCTION

BASIC

INTERMEDIATE

ADVANCED

PILATES FOR YOU

Squeeze your legs together.

Lower and lift your heels together 3 times.

Make sure your body stays in one long line like a plank.

Your heel should point towards the ceiling.

Lower your right heel.

Maintain your abdominal scoop.

ZeSt tip

Keep your stomach scooped and your neck long. Try not to let your head or tummy drop.

Then lift your right heel.

1 From Child's Pose, stretch your legs out long, so you're lying on your stomach, hands under your shoulders, and lift up to a push-up position, fingertips pointing forward, toes tucked under.

2 Squeeze your legs together, imagining them as a single limb, checking you're super-straight.

3 From this position, stretch your heels back, then rock your weight into the balls of your feet, stretching the tendons at the back of your ankles in preparation for the single leg lift. Do this 3 times.

4 Now, lift your left leg off the mat behind you, keeping it straight, with your heel towards the ceiling.

5 Maintaining your abdominal scoop, repeat the rocking motion on the right leg, then lower your lifted leg to switch to the other leg. Each Achilles tendon should get one stretch.

Do 3 on each side alternating your legs each time. On your final rep, flip over to sit down, ready for Leg Pull-up.

13 Leg pull-up

▶▶▶ Challenges your powerhouse, especially your glutes, as well as working your arms and shoulders.

Your body should be in a straight line with your toes pointed.

Scoop your navel towards your spine.

Zest tip

Keep lifting up and out of your wrists and shoulders and imagine a wide belt suspended from the ceiling supporting your buttocks and hips This will help keep them stable.

Kick your right leg up to the ceiling and flex your foot at the top.

★ BEST FOR
EASING TENSION

Point your toe before it touches the mat.

Extend and lengthen your leg from your hip us you lower it.

1 Sit up on your mat, hands by your sides, fingers pointing forward, and lift your hips up so your body is in a straight line, toes pointed.

2 Engage your powerhouse, squeezing your legs together and scooping your navel towards your spine.

3 Inhale and kick your right leg straight up to the ceiling, flexing your foot at the top, pressing your heel away, then exhale, lowering it back down towards the mat with control, pointing your toe before it touches the mat.

4 Change legs to kick the left leg up. Keep alternating until you've done 6.

5 Lower your hips and come to kneel on your mat ready for Kneeling Side Kicks.

▶▶▶ Helps to develop balance and co-ordination, and works the obliques, hips and bottom.

INTRODUCTION

BASIC

INTERMEDIATE

ADVANCED

PILATES FOR YOU

Stretch your left elbow up towards the ceiling.

Keeping your right hip directly above your right knee, lift up your left leg.

Your right hand should be directly underneath your right shoulder.

Keep your powerhouse engaged and your torso firm.

Brush your leg forwards.

Stay long in your head and neck.

Make sure you don't arch your back.

Zest tip

Stay perfectly still in your upper body. Only your leg should be swinging. Don't break at the waist or stick your tail out.

Extend your leg backwards.

1 Kneeling on your mat, bottom raised off your heels, place your right hand on the mat directly under your right shoulder, in line with your knee, fingers pointing to the right.

2 Bend your left elbow, resting your palm behind your head, and stretching your elbow to the ceiling.

3 Extend your left leg out to the side on the mat, then lift it up until it's parallel to the mat, taking care not to wobble and ensuring your powerhouse is engaged, so your torso is firm. Keep your stomach lifted with your back not arched.

4 Brush the extended leg out in front of you, keeping it elevated, and maintaining the strength in your stomach and hips.

5 Exhale as you swing your leg back, still in its elevated position, keeping it long and stretched, while still maintaining the stability in your torso, staying long through your neck and head and drawing your ribs together. Your back shouldn't ache as you do this.

Do 4 kicks with your left leg before swapping to repeat on your right. In your final rep, sit back down to kneeling, ready for Mermaid Side Stretch.

15 Mermaid side stretch

INTRODUCTION

BASIC

INTERMEDIATE

ADVANCED

PILATES FOR YOU

▶▶▶ A balance challenge, this exercise stretches and strengthens the hips and waistline, and works the arms and shoulders.

Stretching the top side of your body.

Zest tip

Try simply holding the position in the beginning, before you advance to lowering and lifting your hips.

Your hand should be directly underneath your shoulder, pressing into the mat for stability. ····

Push up to a long side stretch from your seated mermaid position.

Lower your left arm as you drop your hips slightly.

Stretching the underside of your body.

Bend your right arm over your head in a C-stretch.

Grab hold of your left ankle with your left hand.

1 Sit on your right buttock, knees bent to your left, with your feet stacked one on top of the other, weight resting into your right palm.

2 Ensure your hand is pressing down into the mat, directly underneath your shoulder, lats engaged. Rest your top hand on your shin.

3 Press your weight into your right palm and lift your body up so it forms a straight, diagonal line, engaging your powerhouse to create a rigid line from your heels (feet flexed, one stacked on top of the other) to your head.

4 Take a deep breath in, lifting your left arm straight up over your head, alongside your ear, stretching away from your feet, and lifting your hips. You should feel a lovely stretch along the top side of your body.

5 Lower your left arm down towards your left ankle and exhale slowly, dipping your hips slightly and feeling a stretch along the underside of your body.

6 Keeping your head in line with your spine, lift your hips up once more, lifting your arm up to your ear as before. Repeat this movement 3 times, then sit back down to the mat, grabbing hold of your ankles with your left hand and bending your right arm in a C-stretch over your head, like a mermaid on a rock.

7 Switch to repeat the stretch on your other side, then swing your legs forward to the front of your mat, sitting up tall for Boomerang.

16 Boomerang

▶▶▶ An all-over toner, this stretches and strengthens just about every muscle in your body.

BEST FOR ALL-OVER TONING

Scoop your tummy to lift your legs.

Press your hands into the mat for stability.

Switch your legs over, opening them as wide as your shoulders before closing.

Zesttip
If you feel overwhelmed, imagine you're performing a variation on your Teaser sequence, preceding it with a Roll-over. It helps to break it down in your mind!

Rest your weight on your shoulder blades and not your neck.

Roll back until your legs are overhead.

Raise your arms towards your toes. ....

Roll up to your perfect Teaser position.

Pull your arms back behind you.

Increase the stretch in your shoulders as you lift.

Keep your tummy pulling in and up as you fold forwards.

1 From a seated position, back straight, legs out front and chest lifted, cross your right ankle over your left and press your hands into the mat for stability.

2 Check your stomach is lifted, and roll back until your legs are overhead, pressing your now extended arms into the mat in front of you, palms down. Make sure you rest your weight on your shoulder blades, not your neck.

3 Hold the position as you open your legs and switch them, squeezing your thighs together, so your left is over the right.

4 Roll back up into your Teaser position (see page 71), raising your arms towards your toes then,

moving your arms out behind your body, clasp your hands and stretch them away from your tail.

5 Lower your legs to the mat, scooping your navel towards your spine and rounding over your legs, bringing your nose to your knees with control. Your back should be curled, head bowed. Try to come down in one piece, body over your legs, without crashing.

6 Keep your arms lifted in their clasp position behind your back, then release the clasp, circling your arms towards your feet.

Do 4 reps, switching ankles each time. After your final rep, feed your hands through your legs, ready for Seal.

17 Push-ups

▶▶▶ Fantastic for building strength and definition in your chest, back, shoulders and arms.

INTRODUCTION

BASIC

INTERMEDIATE

ADVANCED

PILATES FOR YOU

★ **BEST FOR**
ARMS AND
SHOULDERS

Scoop your stomach towards your spine.

Your feet should be in Pilates stance.

Zest tip

Make sure you don't drop your hips and sink into your lower back. Your back shouldn't arch, and you should take care not to hang your head. Keep your tummy pulled in and your neck long. Only your arms should be lowering and pushing up.

Roll your body down.

Your body should be straight, in a push-up position.

Your hands should be directly beneath your shoulders.

Keep your legs straight.

Bend your elbows, keeping them tucked in towards your sides.

1 Stand at the back of your mat, feet in Pilates stance, arms stretched up towards the ceiling. Scoop your stomach towards your spine and roll your body down.

2 Walk your hands out down the mat, until they're beneath your shoulders, body straight in a push-up position.

3 Initiate the push up by bending your elbows, keeping them tucked in towards your sides, and lowering your body in a plank until it's hovering a few inches from the mat, ensuring your powerhouse stays strong. Do 3 push-ups, then scoop your stomach to walk your hands back towards your feet, trying not to bend your legs, to increase the stretch. Slowly roll your spine back up until you're standing.

Do 3 reps.

Pilates for you

We've shown you the basic, intermediate and advanced sequences in full. But what if you have limited time and want to target specific problem areas? Or perhaps you have a holiday approaching and want to supplement your mat sequence with a couple of extra targeted workouts that are easy to fit in. That's where our tailored programmes come in. We've created two body-type specific workouts and another for those wanting to target their arms and shoulders. There's also a cool-down de-stress mini-sequence that's ideal for anybody suffering from back or neck pain. It works equally well as a quick counter-stretch at the end of a day in the office.

Assessing body shape

▶▶▶ We can all think of parts of our body that we'd like to work on. Thinking about your body proportions and shape will help you to tailor your Pilates workout to target and improve specific areas.

INTRODUCTION
BASIC
INTERMEDIATE
ADVANCED
PILATES FOR YOU

How to assess your body shape

Broadly speaking, everybody falls into one of two typical body types, referred to as apple or pear shapes. Most people either carry more weight around their middles (apples) or around their bottoms (pears). If you're not sure whether you're an apple or a pear, here are two tests to try:

The tape-measure test

Measure your waist at its narrowest point (no holding it in!). Measure your hips at their widest point (probably just above your pubic line). Divide your waist circumference by your hip circumference. For women, if your score is over 0.80, you're an apple.

As a general guide though (and this is the measurement that doctors follow), the health risks all relate to specific waist measurements. A circumference greater than 80cm (32in) for women and 94cm (37in) for men is the threshold for increased disease risk.

The greatest risk is for women with a waist measurement of more than 88cm (35in) and men with a waist measurement of more than 102cm (40in).

The jiggle test

Stand like the Leonardo da Vinci Vitruvian man – arms outstretched to the side, and legs wide – and wiggle like a belly dancer a few times. As you wiggle, which bits of your body do you feel wobbling the most? If it's your lower body (hips, bottom and thighs), you're likely to be a pear, whereas if it's your stomach, back and arms, you're more likely to be an apple.

YOUR BODY SHAPE AND YOUR HEALTH

Health impacts for apple shapes

In the past decade, huge amounts of scientific data has linked an overweight apple shape with all sorts of health problems. A thick waist (see details in the box) is associated with a higher risk of cardiovascular disease, diabetes and a number of different cancers. This research has caused doctors to reassess advice, focusing on reducing waist-size as equally important as, or even more important than, reducing weight.

The great news for apples reading this book, is that Pilates is an ideal way to reduce your waist circumference as every exercise requires your deep abdominals, transverses, obliques (the muscles that run along the sides of your torso, defining your waist) and rectus (surface) abdominals, to work.

Health impacts for pear shapes

If you're a pear shape then, in health terms, lucky you! Having said that, if you're overweight, you're still at an increased risk of disease, if less so than apples. The targeted plan recommended here will help you to re-balance your body, tapering your hips and thighs so they're more streamlined.

Apple workout

▶ ▶ ▶ This is a must-do workout for anyone seeking to hone their waist and flatten their stomach.

Follow this sequence in order to tackle problem areas if you are an apple shape:

★ Single Leg Stretch (page 34)

★ Double Leg Stretch (page 36)

★ Single Straight Leg Stretch (page 42)

★ Double Straight leg Stretch (page 44)

★ Criss-cross (page 46)

★ Saw (page 52)

★ Spine Twist (page 84)

★ Mermaid Side Stretch (see below for the modified version)

Modified mermaid side stretch

1 Start with your knees bent to the left, sitting on your right buttock, feet stacked one on top of the other. Grab your left shin with your left arm, and curl your right arm overhead, alongside your ear.

2 Instead of lifting up like the Mermaid Side Stretch, stretch down to the mat. Resting on your right elbow, raise your left arm over your head, stretching the left side of your body, then push back up to sitting. Suspend the balance with your arms wide and scoop your belly before repeating the stretch of the right side of your body with your right arm lifted, left arm pulling yourself into a C-shape.

Repeat 3 times.

PROGRESSION If you're feeling adventurous, slide all the way down to the mat lying flat on your side, resting your ear on your extended arm, before returning to sitting.

Pear workout

▶▶▶ A sequence for those with a heavier lower body which helps to streamline your hips, thighs and bottom.

INTRODUCTION

BASIC

INTERMEDIATE

ADVANCED

PILATES FOR YOU

Side clams

1 Lie on your side, shoulders and hips in line, as in your side kick series position (see page 62), then bend your knees, with one leg resting on top of the other, heels in line with your hips.

2 Scoop your stomach towards your spine, then lift your top knee upwards until it's pointing towards the ceiling, keeping your heels tightly pressed together. Return it back down with control. Do this 10 times, rotating the knee upwards by squeezing your glutes and opening your hips.

3 Then lift both feet off the ground with your heels pressed together.

4 Lift your top knee upwards towards the ceiling, keeping your heels pressed together, in an elevated clam. Repeat 10 times.

Zest tip

Keep your heels tightly pressed together to activate the glute connection as your knee rotates.

Pelvic lifts

1 Lie on your back with your knees bent together and feet together on the mat. Your back should be imprinted in the mat.

2 Scooping your navel towards your spine, tilt your pelvis underneath and start to lift your hips off the mat.

3 Keeping your lower back curling, peel your vertebrae one by one off the mat, until you reach a perfect shoulder bridge, no higher.

4 Keep your inner thighs squeezing and buttocks tight. Hold the position, then slowly roll your spine back down bone by bone with control, keeping your abdominal scoop and squeeze.

Do 5 reps, then flip over onto your side, ready for side kick series.

Pear

Side kick series

Do the entire side kick series (see pages 62–7) on the right first, then perform Beating Your Legs or Frog Lifts (or both!) as a transition, before rolling over to change sides, and repeating on your left.

Beating your legs

1 Lying on your stomach, forehead resting on your hands, squeeze your thighs together and wrap your glutes.

2 Inhale, lifting both thighs off the mat, keeping your heels together and your tummy lifted.

3 Then beat your legs together, opening and closing vigorously. Do 10 beats. Return your legs to the mat, then repeat. Do 3 sets, then bend your knees, flexing your toes to the ceiling ready for Frog Lifts (if you are doing both).

Zest tip

Keep working your legs 'long' - out of your hips. Try not to grip your thighs, and don't over-clench your buttocks.

Frog lifts

1 Lying on your stomach as before, bend your knees and flex your feet to the ceiling.

2 Squeezing your heels together tightly and wrapping your glutes, lift your knees up slightly off the mat and lower, 10 times, then repeat. Remember to keep your navel lifting away from the mat.

Squeeze your heels together tightly to wrap your glutes and transform your bottom into a tiny peach!

Banish bingo wings

▶▶▶ This sequence is a must-do for anyone wanting to tone and sculpt a lean and defined upper body.

Push-ups (see page 112)
End by walking your hands back towards your feet, and rolling up to standing, taking a hand weight in each hand (1–1.5kg/2–3lb will be enough).

Then do the Bicep Curls series below. Find the perfect postural position for this series before you start. Standing in Pilates stance, lean forward, as if you were at the top of a ski slope, in one diagonal line, without sticking your tail out. Keep your powerhouse active and the backs of your legs engaged. Maintain this position throughout.

Bicep curls

1 Standing in Pilates stance, extend your arms straight out in front of you at shoulder height, hands grasping your weights and palms to the ceiling.

2 Slowly curl your fists and forearms towards your shoulders, without dropping your elbows, then return them to the start position.

Do 5–8 reps, and finish in your start position, with arms hanging down in front of you, ready for Zip Up.

Zest tip

Maintain your posture throughout. Don't let your tail start to stick out.

1

2a

2b

BICEP CURLS

INTRODUCTION

BASIC

INTERMEDIATE

ADVANCED

PILATES FOR YOU

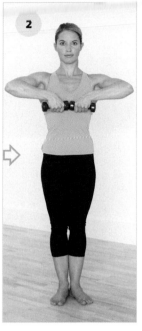

Zip up

1 Stand in Pilates stance, with your arms in front of you, fists facing forwards and weights in your hands, pointing down.

2 Inhale, and scoop your navel to your spine, drawing the weights up your torso as you bend your elbows outwards, as if you were pulling a giant zip up your midline.

3 Exhale, lowering your hands back down with control.

Do 5–8 reps, then return to your start position, ready for Shaving the Head.

Shaving the head

1 Stand in Pilates stance, maintaining your lean and holding your weights behind your head, thumb and forefinger forming a triangle pointing directly upwards.

2 Keeping your shoulders down, press your hands out, diagonally forward, then bring them back down behind your head. Exhale as you push the weights out.

3 Keep your elbows wide, as in line with your ears as possible.

Do 5–8 reps. To finish, move your feet so that they are hip-distance apart and parallel, and fold your upper body over as if you were ready to dive into a pool, ready for Boxing.

Banish bingo wings

Boxing

1 Standing with your knees bent over your toes, body almost parallel to the floor, stomach lifted and weights in each fist, tuck your elbows in to your torso, fists facing one another.

2 Simultaneously extend one arm out in front of you, level with your shoulder and one behind you, also level with your shoulder. Then return your arms in to your sides and swap arms.

Keep alternating for eight. Then return to your start position, ready for Hug.

Hug

1 Bent over, with your upper body hinged forward, knees bent, feet parallel and holding weights, let your arms hang straight down towards the mat.

2 Round your arms as if hugging a large tree. Slowly open your arms wide to the sides, pulling your shoulder blades together and taking care not to arch your back or strain your neck.

Repeat 5–8 times then return to your tree-hug position. Keep your stomach scooped and lats pulling down, before standing upright.

Feeling tense?

▶ ▶ ▶ This simple exercise will help to release back, neck and shoulder tension. Use it at the end of your work day to realign your posture.

Rolling down the wall

1 Stand with your back against the wall, feet in Pilates stance about a step in front of your head, pulling your navel towards your spine to draw your lower back towards the wall.

2 Start to roll your back down, peeling each vertebra away from the wall until only your tailbone is left in contact with the wall, navel pulling inwards and upwards. Let your arms hang in their sockets, circling loosely outwards. Do 3 circles outwards, then 3 inwards. Really relax and let the weight of your arms create the momentum.

3 Stop circling, scoop your belly button back into your spine, and use the scoop to peel yourself up, vertebra by vertebra, returning to the wall, keeping your stomach scooped as you come back up and your shoulders melting down your back. Once upright, take care not to tuck your pelvis under or round your shoulders away from the wall in an effort to get your back flat. Don't worry if it doesn't quite touch, just keep drawing your navel in.

PROGRESSION This exercise can be done holding your weights, to deepen the stretch slightly.

PROGRESSION

Resources & acknowledgements

Further reading...

★ *A Pilates' Primer: Return to Life Through Contrology and Your Health* by Joseph H. Pilates, Presentation Dynamics Inc, 2000

★ *Pilates' Return to Life Through Contrology* by Joseph H. Pilates, Bodymind Publishing, Inc, 1998

★ *The Complete Writings of Joseph H. Pilates*, Bainbridge Books, 2000

★ www.zest.co.uk – expert health, fitness and beauty advice from the number one women's health magazine

Thanks...

With thanks to Yamarama (www.yamarama.com) and Sweaty Betty (www.sweatybetty.com) for supplying clothing.

Index